VOLUME 14 • ISSL

MW00723596

GREAT COMMISSION
RESEARCH JOURNAL

Published by the Great Commission Research Network

Published by the Great Commission Research Network (GCRN)
GCRN's Registered Agent: Corporation Service Company
7716 Old Canton Road, Suite C
Madison, MS 39110

www.greatcommissionresearch.com

Printed in the United States of America by Martel Press, Claremont, CA

Correspondence: 695 E. Bougainvillea St., Azusa, CA 91702 USA

THE PURPOSE of the *Great Commission Research Journal* is to communicate recent thinking and research related to effective church growth and evangelism.

THE JOURNAL The *Great Commission Research Journal* (formerly, *The Journal of the American Society for Church Growth*) is published semi-annually, Fall and Spring. It is indexed in *Christian Periodical Index* and the *Atla Religion Database*.

ISSN 1947-5837 (print)
ISSN 2638-9983 (online)
ISBN 978-1-7377520-0-4

CONTENTS

GREAT COMMISSION
RESEARCH JOURNAL
2022, Vol. 14(1) 5-18

Writing Literature Reviews in Church-Based Research

David R. Dunaetz, Editor

Abstract

Because of the knowledge explosion taking place, literature reviews in church-based research are needed more than ever. Summaries and syntheses of previous research make this knowledge available to practitioners and help researchers focus on what remains unknown. In contrast to empirical studies, literature reviews rely on previously published studies to make conclusions and advance theory. These studies may include both church-based research and more general research that is not particularly Christian. In contrast to meta-analyses which focus on synthesizing statistical information, literature reviews focus on conceptual synthesis and theory advancement. To write a literature review, authors must first choose a research problem to address. An initial review of past literature will help them focus on a narrower research question, most likely in an iterative process, to choose a specific topic. The authors must also consider the purpose of their review in light of past research and theoretical contributions that they can make to the chosen topic.

The knowledge explosion of the last several decades has produced unprecedented quantities of evidence-based research, including research that is relevant to evangelism, disciple making, and virtually all church-based ministries (Cooper, 1988; Dunaetz, 2020a; Grant & Booth, 2009). In the social sciences and other fields that focus on understanding humans (e.g., church-based research), the explosion is especially notable because of the complexity of human behavior (Adair & Vohra, 2003). Most empirical studies in these fields focus on a very specific phenomenon, resulting in a broad range of studies, each touching on a narrow aspect of how humans act in different situations and contexts. Since the 1980s, researchers have been overloaded with information, resulting in an increased sense of need for literature reviews that summarize and synthesize the many streams of research in a given field (Cooper, 1988). Literature reviews not only play an essential role in the dissemination of research, but they also help researchers avoid unnecessary duplication of effort and allow them to build upon the work of those who have gone before them (Bordens & Abbott, 2011).

A literature review that summarizes and synthesizes research can provide the reader with an easily accessible overview of the advances that have occurred in a field, for example, Fapohunda's (2021) review of the theological literature on integrity and evangelism. This summary and synthesis approach may be the most common approach taken by scholars in seminaries and theological schools. But literature reviews can also provide a bridge between specialized fields, such as linking research in organizational psychology and church-based research. For example, literature reviews have been used to summarize research on organizational justice (the perception of being fairly or unfairly treated; Colquitt et al., 2001; Cropanzano & Ambrose, 2015) that can be applied to Christian organizations (Dunaetz, 2010) and to church planting (Dunaetz, 2020b). This is similar to Augustine's use of platonic philosophy for Christian purposes in accord with Scripture, described with the metaphor of the Israelites plundering the Egyptians during the Exodus (Augustine, 397, Book 2, Chapter 40). In addition, literature reviews may be undertaken in preparation for additional research (Grant & Booth, 2009; Paré et al., 2015). A review can identify gaps that exist in our knowledge of a topic. These gaps can form the basis of research questions.

With the general purposes of literature reviews in mind, we can address some of the steps involved in writing literature reviews that will be beneficial to both researchers and practitioners.

Choosing a Topic

Before writing a literature review, researchers must begin with a topic that they consider important. In church-based research, this topic may come from personal experiences (e.g., Hilderbrand, 2022, in this issue), previous research that piqued the author's interest, theories that seem relevant to ministry, or from real-life problems (Bordens & Abbott, 2011). Concern about deconversions (Streib, 2021), ethics and evangelism (Fapohunda, 2021), measuring church attendance (Smith, 1998), and the meaning of church health (Huizing, 2012) have all led to literature reviews relevant to ministry.

But a topic should not be studied and reviewed simply because it has been researched previously. A good literature review, as with all solid research, will address a research problem, some problem that does not yet have a definitive solution and is considered important by at least some people. The research problem should not be something trivial or a simple repeat of what has been addressed previously. The problem should be of manageable size so that any answers or hypotheses that emerge from the literature review can be tested (Salkind, 2017). Yet the research problem should be important enough to justify the effort needed to find a solution.

Once the research problem is at least tentatively identified, one or more research questions can be formed (Bordens & Abbott, 2011; Dunaetz, 2020c; Salkind, 2017). A research question is a question whose answer will at least provide a partial solution to the research problem. The answer to a research question might not solve the research problem completely, but it at least contributes some knowledge relevant to the problem, even if it raises more questions than it answers.

A good research question needs to be answerable (Bordens & Abbott, 2011). This often means that an answer can be developed empirically, that is, collectible data should conceivably provide evidence for a valid answer to the research question. Although purely philosophical research questions may be addressed without data, most answers to church-focused research questions are more convincing when data exists. At the broadest level, this data might be what biblical texts say about the topic, or what theologians have said about it. But for more practical problems, qualitative and quantitative data are likely to provide new insights into specific church-based phenomena in contemporary contexts. A literature review should not just cover the theological aspects of a research question, but also the empirical studies that have been conducted. Qualitative church-based studies tend to collect data from interviews (e.g., Moon, 2020) or from ethnographic observations (e.g., Ward, 2015). Quantitative church-based studies tend to collect data from surveys (e.g., Bocala-Wiedemann, 2022, in this issue).

A good research question will also provide the rationale for a literature review. It will address some need that is felt by others rather than simply be an expression of the author's interest or curiosity. It will be presented in such a way as to explain why this is an important question, relevant to people's lives either in or outside of the Christian community. It will also be framed in such a way as to address existing contradictions or holes in the church-based literature (Torraco, 2005).

A literature review addressing a research question will not simply be a summary of previous research. Rather, it will lead to something new, such as a hypothesis that can be tested, a theory that integrates the previous research, or a proposal for additional research to address what the existing literature cannot address. However, we often do not begin research with a literature review. We tend to start with a research question, and based on our experience, we come up with a hypothesis. Then we conduct a literature review based on the variables or phenomena found in our hypothesis. We tend to think that this will be a linear process (Dunaetz, 2020c):

Research Question ➡ Hypothesis or Theory ➡ Literature Review

However, this is not a linear process. Once we examine the literature, we often discover something that will modify the research question or the hypothesis, perhaps several times. Developing a research question, hypothesis, and literature is often an iterative process, which can be better represented as:

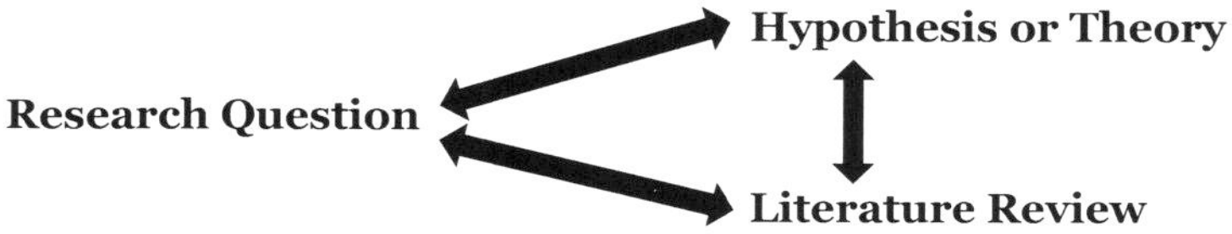

This nonlinear process can be frustrating, often leading to major revisions in both our thinking and our manuscript. However, it is a necessary process to fully integrate the literature into our thinking and to produce a valuable literature review that can provide useful information (Salkind, 2017).

Writing the Literature Review

The Structure Depends on the Purpose

The purpose of the literature review will greatly influence both the structure of the review and the choice of literature to include (Bem, 1995). For example, if the author is trying to summarize competing models or theories (e.g., missional communities, Urton, 2022, in this issue) to make a conclusion about the best or most relevant in a given situation or to propose a better one, the literature review will be structured around the various models or theories.

If the author's goal is to promote a specific or novel view (e.g., Davison, 2022, in this issue), the author might begin with a description of the conventional view and why it is widely accepted. The author may then explore studies that either support or do not support the conventional view. The author may then synthesize this information, making either an improvement to the conventional view or presenting a new, more comprehensive view.

If the purpose of a review is to lead up to a testable hypothesis, then the review may be structured around the two or more variables invoked in the hypothesis. For each variable, the various definitions that are found in the literature, the demonstrated antecedents of that variable, and the demonstrated consequences of that variable should be reviewed. The conclusion of the review should logically lead to the hypothesis to be tested. For example, if an initial review of the relevant literature leads to the hypothesis, "The greater the cultural homogeneity, the faster a newly planted church will grow, especially when the age of the members is relatively low," the three variables to include in the review would be cultural homogeneity, church growth, and the age of church members.

To structure the review so that it logically leads to the hypothesis to be tested, the reviewer can begin (after an appropriate introduction presenting the research problem or question) with an in-depth discussion of cultural homogeneity (and its opposite, cultural diversity). This would include discussing the various definitions and measures of cultural diversity, specifying the definition and operationalization (a way it can be measured) chosen for this study. The review would also include the research that has uncovered antecedents (e.g., causes) of cultural homogeneity or diversity and the research that has uncovered consequences (e.g., results) of cultural homogeneity or diversity. The literature review should not be limited to the research done on cultural homogeneity in the church but should cover the whole range of literature that may be relevant. After reviewing cultural diversity, the author should include similarly structured sections on church growth and the age of church members. All three concepts should be logically tied together in the conclusion, resulting in a hypothesis that can be tested empirically.

The logic of a literature review for such a study can be summarized roughly in broad terms as "There's a problem with A. It appears to be related to B and C. Here's what we know about A (its definition, antecedents, and consequences). Here's what we know about B (its definition, antecedents, and consequences). Here's what we know about C (its definition, antecedents, and consequences). Putting this all together, we can propose that A, B, and C are related in such-and-such a way. To remove any doubt, we will collect data to see if it fits this proposal."

Choosing the Appropriate Sources

When writing a literature review, it is important to find all the relevant literature, sort through it, reject the low-quality material, and focus on what is left (Grant & Booth, 2009). When describing research-relevant literature, it is useful to classify each work as a primary, secondary, or tertiary source (Salkind, 2017).

Primary sources are original, empirical studies that collect data to test a hypothesis, form a theory, or describe a phenomenon. Most primary research is reported in peer-reviewed journals (e.g., *Great Commission Research Journal, Christian Education Journal, Missiology: An International Review*, or *Psychology of Religion and Spirituality*) and has sections introducing the problem examined, a literature review, hypotheses or research questions, a description of the methods used to collect the data, the results of an analysis of the data, a discussion of the meaning and implications of the results, and a list of references used in the study. Some edited books also contain primary sources. Books edited by academics (e.g., Ireland & Raven, 2020; Wuthnow, 1994) with chapters written by different specialists also may report primary research, although other chapters would be considered secondary sources.

Secondary sources are compilations and summaries of primary research. These may take the form of a book written by a researcher (e.g., McGavran & Wagner, 1990; Twenge, 2017b), literature reviews (such as those mentioned previously), meta-analyses (statistical summaries of quantitative studies, e.g., Donahue, 1985; Mahoney et al., 2021), handbooks (collections of review articles written by scholars on a specific topic, e.g., Davis, 2010; Hunt, 2019), and sometimes review articles written by experts in serious magazines such *The Atlantic* and *Harvard Business Review* (e.g., Maccoby, 2000; Twenge, 2017a).

All other sources are tertiary sources. These include popular books based on the author's experience or opinion, encyclopedias, textbooks, newspapers, Wikipedia, popular magazines such as *Christianity Today* or *Psychology Today*, and most web pages. Tertiary (or general) sources are useful for getting an overview of the topic or for demonstrating the reality and importance of a problem, but they are not considered credible scholarly resources and should generally not be included in literature reviews. Rather, literature reviews should focus on primary and secondary sources.

It is essential to focus on high-quality sources. The internet has made it easier to access high-quality research easily and freely through sites like ResearchGate.net, Academia.edu, and Scholar.Google.com. However, it has also made it easier to disseminate low-quality research as well. High-quality sources of research are generally found in peer-reviewed journals with editors and reviewers who are academic experts in their fields. An easy, but not sufficient, way to identify peer-reviewed scholarship is to look for an abstract at the beginning of the article. Most peer-reviewed articles begin with an abstract that can help the reader determine if the rest of the article is worth reading. An abstract generally contains a summary of the article, including a description of the sample used in the study, the research methods used to conduct the research, and a summary of the results (i.e., it is not a teaser to motivate you to read more). The website of the journal publisher should provide information about the editorial board and the peer-review process used to select papers to publish.

The researcher should try to use the highest quality research when preparing a literature review. Some journals, usually among the oldest in their field, are more selective in what they publish than other journals. Authors often submit their work to one of these more prestigious journals first and then, if their work is rejected at their first choice, resubmit to less prestigious journals until it is accepted somewhere. The prestige of a journal is mainly determined by its impact factor, the average number of times per year articles from that journal are cited by other journals (see mjl.clarivate.com for one measure of the impact factor of thousands of journals). The general importance of a specific article is measured by the number of times it has been cited by other scholarly works; Google scholar (scholar.google.com) provides an easily accessible approximation of these citations for each article, as well as a searchable database of journal rankings based on what Google calls the h5-index (https://scholar.google.com/citations?view_op=metrics_intro).

Unfortunately, the last decade has seen an explosion of poor research published in what has come to be known as predatory journals (Beall, 2015). Because academics must often publish or perish, a market has developed for publishing low-quality journals. Academics are spammed daily with invitations to publish in supposedly peer-reviewed journals with publishing fees that range from tens to thousands of dollars. These journals typically have legitimate-sounding names but will publish most any paper for the publishing fee. These journals are typically "open access," that is, freely accessible on the web immediately upon publication. There are some legitimate open access journals because some funders require it (e.g., *PLOS One*, *SAGE Open*), but many are predatory. Since new predatory journals appear regularly, there is no list that identifies all of them (and some of the older lists mistakenly included legitimate journals in them). Here are some guidelines for determining if a journal is legitimate.

- Google the name of the journal (in quotation marks) plus "predatory." The journal may appear in a list of known predatory journals.
- Check out the publisher. Legitimate journals are usually published by large, well-known publishers (e.g., Wiley, Sage, Elsevier, Blackwell, Cambridge University Press, Emerald) or by not-for-profit professional societies that are focused on a specific topic (e.g., Great Commission Research Network, Evangelical Missiological Society, American Psychological Association). Again, google the name of the journal (in quotation marks) plus "predatory" and examine the results.
- Examine the number of citations the article has received. In Google Scholar (scholar.google.com), find the article and the "Cited by" number on the final line of the article description. Low-quality articles from predatory journals are rarely cited (at least not by scholars; students are less selective.)

Not all low-quality research is found in predatory journals. When journals are first launched, they may have difficulty attracting high-quality submissions and have to publish the best that they have, even if the research is not especially credible or insightful. Unlike predatory journals, these journals may have a legitimate peer-review system and may not charge publication fees. They are sometimes known as "emerging sources" (Clarivate, 2022) and are often published in developing countries where universities are growing and trying to establish international reputations (often by adopting Western "publish or perish" norms in academia). Signs of low-quality research include poor English editing, poor typesetting, the use of weak evidence or arguments, vague information about the research methods used, and the improper use of statistics. When writing literature reviews, researchers need to critically examine each source of information to be included in the review.

Types of Literature Reviews

Literature reviews can have different forms and purposes (Cooper, 1988; Grant & Booth, 2009; Paré et al., 2015). All of them result from the authors "locating, obtaining, reading, and evaluating the research literature" (Bordens & Abbot, 2011, p. 66) relevant to their research question. Literature reviews are distinct from empirical studies in that literature reviews do not seek to collect new data concerning a specific phenomenon. Whereas empirical studies tend to have narrow research questions, literature reviews can have broader research questions that are addressed by integrating the results of a wide range of empirical and theoretical studies (Baumeister & Leary, 1997). Literature reviews are also distinct from meta-analyses (Glass, 1976; Rosenthal & DiMatteo, 2001), which are summaries of quantitative studies with the results presented in tables of numbers (Baumeister & Leary, 1997). Meta-analyses serve similar functions as literature reviews and can be just as (or even more) informative than them. Meta-analyses help sort through contradictory studies which find both significant and insignificant relationships between variables by combining the statistics presented in the individual articles into a composite calculation of the strength of the relationship. The meta-analysis presents a conclusion that is more trustworthy than the conclusions of individual studies included. Meta-analyses can also discover moderating variables, that is, conditions under which a relationship is especially strong or does not exist (Rosenthal, 1991; Rosenthal & DiMatteo, 2001).

The Purpose of the Literature Review

The purpose of the literature review should be clear to the author from the beginning because it will influence every aspect of the research process. There are many different ways of classifying literature reviews by their purpose (Cooper, 1988; Grant & Booth, 2009; Paré et al., 2015). Some of the most common are described as follows.

Critical Reviews. The purpose of critical reviews is to demonstrate that the author has mastered the literature on the topics relevant to the research question and to provide the background necessary to do additional research (Dunaetz, 2020c; Grant & Booth, 2009). These reviews typically result in a hypothesis or a model to be tested. This is the most common type of review written by graduate students as they prepare their thesis or dissertation. They are also found in the introduction to empirical studies to provide the background necessary to understand the research and to provide justification for the hypothesis tested or research question addressed.

Narrative Reviews. The purpose of narrative reviews (e.g., Mermilliod, 2021) is to summarize the most important research on a topic (Baumeister & Leary, 1997; Grant & Booth, 2009). They present what is known and what is not known on a topic. These reviews often occur in academic journals with "review" in the title.

Systematic Reviews. These reviews focus (e.g., Fapohunda, 2021) on a systematic search of all the databases for knowledge on a topic (Fehrmann & Hawkins, 2014; Fehrmann & Wagner, 2012; Grant & Booth, 2009). The standard for the search is often set by an external authority, such as a funder or a doctoral advisor. In principle, systematic reviews done by different researchers will yield similar conclusions.

Integrative Reviews. Also known as theory development reviews, integrative reviews seek to tie various strands of research together into a coherent whole, such as a modification of an existing theory or into a new theory, or to apply knowledge from one field to another field (Baumeister & Leary, 1997; Torraco, 2005). Integrative reviews are typically used when research done in secular contexts is applied to Christian contexts (e.g., Dunaetz, 2010) or when research done in one ministry context is reviewed and applied to another ministry context (e.g., Urton, 2022). Integrative reviews are especially relevant for application-focused research journals such as the *Great Commission Research Journal.*

Factors to Consider When Writing a Literature Review

The form of a literature review will depend on many choices that the author must make. The SALSA framework for literature reviews (Search, Appraisal, Synthesis, and Analysis; Grant & Booth, 2009) describes some of the main choices.

Search. How will the researcher find relevant articles and how much time will be invested in finding these articles? Using the academic databases in libraries (Atla Religion, PsychInfo, ProQuest Religion, etc.) allows for a systematic approach to searching for literature that can be reproduced (e.g., Fapohunda, 2021), but it tends to be slow and the order in which the works are presented is not always clear. Google Scholar (scholar.google.com) is much faster. It sorts the results first by the number of keywords in the title and then by the number of times the work has been cited. But Google Scholar can produce different results at different times and contains more irrelevant results. Library databases require some sort of membership or affiliation, but Google Scholar often has direct download links to PDFs in the right column next to each work. Google Scholar is also linkable to university libraries and databases (via Settings) to download articles when PDFs are not available for direct download.

AppraisaL. To what degree will the literature review appraise and evaluate the works included? Sometimes the appraisal is done informally to determine what works the researcher wants to read more thoroughly. In this case, no appraisal of the quality of the research is presented in the published literature review. This may be the case when a limited number of works are being compared (e.g., Urton, 2022, in this issue). Other times, the researcher may evaluate the methods used in each article and only report relevant conclusions based on the high-quality studies. In other studies, the researcher may want to provide information on the quality of all the studies examined, both high and low to compare and contrast the high- and low-quality studies (e.g., Stewart et al., 2010).

Synthesis. Putting the information together from various studies examined can take on several forms. Sometimes the researcher just wants to introduce research on a topic without trying to synthesize it. But more often, especially in more detailed literature reviews, a more complete synthesis is needed. The most common form of synthesis is a narrative integrating all that is known about the phenomenon under consideration. This calls for a mastery of the relevant research and insight into how to present it coherently. Other times, a historical synthesis is appropriate, presenting a chronological description of how knowledge and perception of a phenomenon have evolved to the present state. In other cases, the synthesis can be put in tabular form, especially if the information can be presented in a clear and logical structure that has little need for a narrative explanation.

Analysis. In most cases, the researcher writes a literature review to lead to new ideas, perhaps a new theory, perhaps a new application of a theory, perhaps a research question to be addressed, perhaps a hypothesis to be tested. To do so, the literature reviewed must be analyzed. When creating a new theory or a new application of a theory, the analysis needs to be in-depth and robust. When trying to describe the current state of research to determine what is known and what is unknown to justify further research, the literature review needs to be complete, but the analysis presented may be shorter than in other types of literature reviews.

These are the main factors that should be taken into consideration when writing a literature review (Grant & Booth, 2009). Other factors should also be taken into consideration (Cooper, 1988; Paré et al., 2015), including the audience who is likely to read the review (generalist or specialist), the scope of the review (broad or narrow), and overall focus (theory, research methods, or practice). All of these factors should be considered when writing a literature view.

Practical Guidelines

To make a literature review as useful as possible to the audience who might find it either through searching library databases or the web, following several practical guidelines can help.

Accessibility. Anyone with a college education should be able to read a well-written literature review (Bem, 1995). It should not be addressed to specialists, so specialized vocabulary needs to be explained. The specialized vocabulary associated with different fields of church-based research is useful among specialists (e.g., homogenous unit, catalyst, or movement), but needs to be explained so that those who are not familiar with the technical meaning of an expression can understand the review.

Avoiding Lists. Most humans would rather read a story than a phonebook. A literature review should aim at telling a story, communicating a central idea in a persuasive manner (Bem, 1995; Sternberg, 1991). Authors should avoid mind-numbing lists and bullet points. They should argue for a clear point of view, creating a flow that is natural and coherent, with adjacent ideas clearly linked. They need to stay focused on the argument, avoiding tangents. In literature reviews, it is easy to get distracted by describing relatively unimportant research.

Clarity. Clarity and precision are primordial for literature reviews, whereas flare and style should be secondary (Bem, 1995). Figurative and ambiguous language should be avoided. Accuracy is more important than using a wide vocabulary or flowery constructions. Parallel structure in sentences and paragraphs is especially useful for this. For example, suppose I want to communicate two ideas. The first is: When a youth pastor arrives in a church that is under 5 years old, such a church tends to grow when the neighborhood is growing. The second idea can be communicated either as:

1) When a new head pastor arrives in a church under 5 years old, such a church tends not to grow even if the neighborhood is growing.
2) In growing neighborhoods, church growth does not result from the installation of a new head pastor if the church is under 5 years old.

Standing alone, sentences 1) and 2) are about equally clear concerning the second idea. But given the first idea, sentence 1) is much clearer because it maintains the same structure and makes it easy to understand the contrast made. Parallel structure makes both contrasts and comparisons easier to understand.

Write and Rewrite. Few writers put their thoughts onto paper clearly in their first attempt. We need to write, rewrite, and rewrite some more until the text is as clear and precise as we can make it (Bem, 1995). Once we have gotten that far, we should give our manuscript to one or more of our most critical, trusted colleagues (perhaps even our spouse) and ask them to critique it. If they say something is unclear, we should believe them and continue improving it. When we submit our literature review to a peer-reviewed journal, the reviewers will likely find even more issues that need addressing. This is all part of producing the highest quality research. We should embrace it rather than fight against it.

Conclusion

Literature reviews are an essential tool for dealing with the explosion of knowledge relevant to church-based research. They may be difficult and time-consuming to write, but they can serve all those seeking to fulfill the Great Commission by summarizing and synthesizing information that may enable them to be more effective. May the readers of the *Great Commission Research Journal* be motivated to write more literature reviews and may the literature reviews published in the journal contribute to the advancement of the Kingdom of God.

David R. Dunaetz, Editor
ddunaetz@apu.edu

References

Adair, J. G., & Vohra, N. (2003). The explosion of knowledge, references, and citations: Psychology's unique response to a crisis. *American Psychologist, 58*(1), 15-23.

Augustine. (397). *On Christian doctrine.*

Baumeister, R. F., & Leary, M. R. (1997). Writing narrative literature reviews. *Review of General Psychology, 1*(3), 311-320.

Beall, J. (2015). Predatory journals and the breakdown of research cultures. *Information Development, 31*(5), 473-476.

Bem, D. J. (1995). Writing a review article for Psychological Bulletin. *Psychological Bulletin, 118*(2), 172-177.

Bocala-Wiedemann, T. J. (2022). Social media as a tool for evangelism among youth and young adults. *Great Commission Research Journal, 14*(1), 19-34.

Bordens, K. S., & Abbott, B. B. (2011). *Research design and methods: A process approach* (8th ed.). Mc Graw-Hill.

Clarivate. (2022). *Web of science: Emerging sources citation index.* https://clarivate.com/webofsciencegroup/solutions/webofscience-esci/

Colquitt, J. A., Conlon, D. E., Wesson, M. J., Porter, C., & Ng, K. Y. (2001). Justice at the millennium: A meta-analytic review of 25 years of organizational justice research. *Journal of Applied Psychology, 86*(3), 425-445.

Cooper, H. M. (1988). Organizing knowledge syntheses: A taxonomy of literature reviews. *Knowledge in Society, 1*(1), 104-126.

Cropanzano, R., & Ambrose, M. L. (2015). Organizational justice: Where we have been and where we are going. In R. Cropanzano & M. L. Ambrose (Eds.), *The Oxford handbook of justice in the workplace* (pp. 3-14). Oxford University Press.

Davis, D. H. (2010). *The Oxford handbook of church and state in the United States.* Oxford University Press.

Davison, J. (2022). The continuity mindset for Christian mission. *Great Commission Research Journal, 14*(1), 51-68.

Donahue, M. J. (1985). Intrinsic and extrinsic religiousness: Review and meta-analysis. *Journal of Personality and Social Psychology, 48*(2), 400-419.

Dunaetz, D. R. (2010). Organizational justice: Perceptions of being fairly treated. In D. Baker & D. Hayward (Eds.), *Serving Jesus with integrity: Ethics and accountability in mission* (pp. 197-221). William Carey Library.

Dunaetz, D. R. (2020a). Church-based research: Challenges and opportunities. *Great Commission Research Journal, 12*(1), 1-17.

Dunaetz, D. R. (2020b). Organizational justice in young churches: Maximizing fair treatment of others and responding to violations. *Jurnal Jaffray, 18*(1), 1-19.

Dunaetz, D. R. (2020c). *Research methods and survey applications: Outlines and activities from a Christian perspective* (3rd ed.). Martel Press.

Fapohunda, B. (2021). The role of personal integrity in soulwinning: A systematic review of the theological literature. *The Evangelical Review of Theology and Politics, 9*, 37-54.

Fehrmann, P., & Hawkins, M. (2014). Using rapid review methods for topics in religion. *Advances in the Study of Information and Religion, 4*(2014), Article 4.

Fehrmann, P., & Wagner, S. H. (2012). A systematic literature review model for religion. https://oaks.kent.edu/node/261

Glass, G. V. (1976). Primary, secondary, and meta-analysis of research. *Educational Researcher, 5*(10), 3-8.

Grant, M. J., & Booth, A. (2009). A typology of reviews: An analysis of 14 review types and associated methodologies. *Health Information & Libraries Journal, 26*(2), 91-108.

Hilderbrand, K. M. (2022). The sinner's prayer: An inappropriate ritual for Thai Christian culture and a suggested replacement. *Great Commission Research Journal, 14*(1), 69-85.

Huizing, R. (2012). In search of the healthy church: A meta-ethnographic study. *Great Commission Research Journal, 4*(1), 43-59.

Hunt, S. (Ed.). (2019). *Handbook of megachurches*. Brill.

Ireland, J., & Raven, M. (Eds.). (2020). *Practicing hope: Missions in goblal crises.* William Carey Publishing.

Maccoby, M. (2000). Narcissistic leaders: The incredible pros, the inevitable cons. *Harvard Business Review, 78*(1), 68-78.

Mahoney, A., Wong, S., Pomerleau, J. M., & Pargament, K. I. (2021). Sanctification of diverse aspects of life and psychosocial functioning: A meta-analysis of studies from 1999 to 2019. *Psychology of Religion and Spirituality*, Advance online publication. https://doi.org/https://psycnet.apa.org/doi/10.1037/rel0000354

McGavran, D. A., & Wagner, C. P. (1990). *Understanding Church Growth* (Third ed.). Eerdmans.

Mermilliod, E. P. (2021). A synthesis of academic research related to church-based family ministry. *Christian Education Journal, 18*(3), 406-423.

Moon, W. J. (2020). Alternative financial models for churches and church plants: When tithes and offerings are not enough. *Great Commission Research Journal, 12*(1), 19-42.

Paré, G., Trudel, M.-C., Jaana, M., & Kitsiou, S. (2015). Synthesizing information systems knowledge: A typology of literature reviews. *Information & Management, 52*(2), 183-199.

Rosenthal, R. (1991). *Meta-analytic procedures for social research*. Sage.

Rosenthal, R., & DiMatteo, M. R. (2001). Meta-analysis: Recent developments in quantitative methods for literature reviews. *Annual Review of Psychology, 52*(1), 59-82.

Salkind, N. J. (2017). *Exploring research* (9th ed.). Pearson.

Smith, T. W. (1998). A review of church attendance measures. *American Sociological Review*, 131-136.

Sternberg, R. J. (1991). Editorial. *Psychological Bulletin, 109*(1), 3-4.

Stewart, R., Van Rooyen, C., Dickson, K., Majoro, M., & De Wet, T. (2010). *What is the impact of microfinance on poor people?: A systematic review of evidence from sub-saharan Africa*. University of London.

Streib, H. (2021). Leaving religion: Deconversion. *Current Opinion in Psychology, 40*, 139-144.

Torraco, R. J. (2005). Writing integrative literature reviews: Guidelines and examples. *Human Resource Development Review, 4*(3), 356-367.

Twenge, J. M. (2017a). Have smartphones destroyed a generation? *The Atlantic*. https://www.theatlantic.com/magazine/archive/2017/09/has-the-smartphone-destroyed-a-generation/534198/

Twenge, J. M. (2017b). *iGen: Why today's super-connected kids are growing up less rebellious, more tolerant, less happy--and completely unprepared for adulthood--and what that means for the rest of us*. Simon and Schuster.

Urton, M. (2022). An examination of three models of missional communities for sharing the gospel with Muslims in the United States. *Great Commission Research Journal, 14*(1), 35-49.

Ward, M. (2015). The powerpoint and the glory: An ethnography of pulpit media and its organizational impacts. *Journal of Media and Religion, 14*(4), 175-195.

Wuthnow, R. (1994). *"I come away stronger": How small groups are shaping American religion*. Wm. B. Eerdmans Publishing.

GREAT COMMISSION
RESEARCH JOURNAL
2022, Vol. 14(1) 19-34

Social Media as a Tool for Evangelism Among Youth and Young Adults

Trisney J. Bocala-Wiedemann
Southern Adventist University

Abstract

This research aims to answer the question of which social media platforms youth prefer and what types of content they prefer. Using data collected from a quantitative survey of Seventh-day Adventist schools, this research seeks to identify the most-used social media platforms and most appealing types of content so Christian churches, media organizations, and digital missionaries can more effectively utilize social media as a tool for evangelism among youth and young adults, defined as people 15 to 24 years of age.

Introduction

In Matthew 28:19, Jesus gave His disciples a Great Commission saying, "Therefore go and make disciples of all nations, baptizing them in the name of the Father, and of the Son, and of the Holy Spirit." Today, 2,000 years later, the Christian church faces the challenge of how to effectively continue this mission as the means of communication evolve.

Literature Review

To understand how to respond to the current cultural context, this literature review synthesizes several sources of research in the area of religion and new media. Previous reviews have explored the communication methods employed by the Seventh-day Adventist (SDA) Church to spread its message throughout history, and whether or not social media has become as popular of a communication channel for churches and religious topics as it has for other organizations and social issues (Reddy, 2019; Tudor & Herteliu, 2016). This literature review examines two main themes: first, the SDA Church's predominant use of traditional media and underutilization of new media, and second, the growth of social media use and the need to invest in digital evangelism on such platforms.

The uses and gratifications theory of media selection, which was chosen as the theoretical framework for this research, was first introduced by Elihu Katz (Katz et al., 1973). Previously, audiences were thought of simply as passive consumers of the media. However, this theory proposes that people choose to consume specific media to fulfill needs unique to each individual. This means that the audience members actively control what information they consume and for what purposes.

Use of Traditional Media

The SDA Church has made thorough use of traditional media but has underutilized newer technology, like social media, in spreading its message. Mike Megrove Reddy (2019) presented compelling statistics for the SDA Church's early growth and its use of various forms of communication. "The Seventh-day Adventist Church maximized all types of communication in order to spread and sustain their values and beliefs" (Reddy 2019, p. 9). Reddy accounts for 25,769 literature evangelists, 62 publishing houses and branches, 20 radio stations, 15 television stations, 9 major internet websites, and 3 media production houses, as of 2014. However, the only mention of the SDA church's social media use in Reddy's (2019) research was the existence of a few official church accounts. Further, Reddy did not conduct an analysis studying the levels of engagement with any known social media accounts, and no conclusion was reached concerning their effectiveness in reaching their intended audiences.

Mihaela-Alexandra Tudor and Agnos-Millian Herteliu (2016) studied the European country with the largest SDA membership, Romania (Reddy, 2019). Their survey sought to find out "whether the dissemination of the Adventist religious spiritual message in general is adapted to the contemporary level of technological development" (Tudor & Herteliu 2016, p. 212). The survey revealed that printed materials are still preferred by Romanian clergy for devotionals, Sabbath School, and sermon preparation. However, they have utilized new media platforms such as livestreams, YouTube, and Facebook for broadcasting evangelistic programs. Tudor and Herteliu also found that while 96.8% of the Romanian SDA Church leaders used Facebook, only 6.5% used Instagram (2016).

Tudor and Herteliu also explained that "the practice of sharing one's personal faith experiences is very common among Christians, as the Bible encourages it in order to strengthen one another in faith" (2016). However, their research found that only 21% use the internet regularly (at least once a week) to promote religion, and only 9% share their faith experiences online. David R. Dunaetz (2019) introduced the Mum Effect as a viable explanation for why social media is not more widely used to spread the gospel. The Mum Effect occurs when a person is reluctant to share bad news. This is often due to the instinct to protect one's reputation. According to Dunaetz, given the pervasive negative stereotypes on social media about Christians, many of them are reluctant to share their faith publicly online. This, in light of Tudor and Herteliu's (2016) research, suggests that Reddy's (2019) conclusion that the SDA Church has successfully utilized various forms of communication to spread the gospel is incomplete, as it fails to recognize the potential still to be gained from social media.

The 2017-2018 SDA Global Church Member Survey indicated that 46% of SDA Church members in the North American Division never engage with SDA social media, 57% of SDA Church members never read or respond to Christian social media of any denomination, and 45% of SDA Church members use social media multiple times per day (North America Division, 2018). At first, this may seem to suggest that social media is not an effective tool for evangelism since fewer than half of the church members regularly use it. However, these statistics are not shocking considering that the average age of an SDA church member in the U.S. is 50 years and the majority of social media users are younger (McChesney, 2016).

In another study, Emmanuel-Lugard Nduka and John McGuire (2017) found five themes among Catholic college students, three of which are highly relevant to this research: 1) the everyday use of new media, 2) the Catholic Church's emphasis on tradition, and 3) failure to program toward youth. The first of these themes focuses on the prevalence of technology in the lives of college-age young adults. Nduka and McGuire (2017) found that the Catholic college students in their sample would like the Catholic Church's message to be disseminated "in [their] language." The second of these themes is that the Catholic Church seems to be "buried in tradition." This aligns with Dunaetz's (2019) research, which concluded that social media and other forms of new media are not regularly used to address religious topics. The third theme was that the Catholic Church failed to cater the message to the college age group. The messages "need to be directed toward young adults specifically in order to captivate their interest and hold their attention" (p. 8).

Growth of Social Media Use

While such research points to the unfilled potential of social media as a tool for evangelism, other research demonstrates why it is important to use social media to spread the gospel. According to the media richness theory developed by Richard L. Daft and Robert H. Lengel (1984), various forms of media can be placed along a richness continuum, measuring various factors such as the speed of feedback and the ability to present uniquely tailored messages. In light of the uses and gratifications theory of media selection, John Carlson (1999) added to this, developing the channel expansion theory which explains that different people perceive different channels for communication "richer" than other forms of media.

Research by Common Sense Media found that the percentage of teenagers who reported using social media multiple times per day increased from 34% to 70% between 2012 and 2018 (Richter, 2018). Presumably, the widespread use of social media among teenagers would indicate that this demographic perceives social media as having greater media richness than older people perceive it to have, and thus a greater possibility of fulfilling this demographic's needs, according to the uses and gratifications theory. Lance Strate (2017) adds insight to this in his analysis of Marshall McLuhan's book *Understanding Media*. Strate (2017) observed, "We generally ignore the medium or technology and only pay attention to its content or the way that it is used, but it is the medium that has the greater impact" (p. 1). Given social media's potential high level of information richness and the importance of selecting an effective medium for a message, it is crucial for churches to utilize social media for evangelism among youth.

Amanda Ratcliff and her colleagues (2017) analyzed people's use of social media to satisfy their religious needs in light of the uses and gratifications theory. They found that positive attitudes toward social media decreased as religiosity increased. This would indicate that those with a lower level of self-reported religiosity are the ones who use social media more frequently and consistently. This is the precise group that needs to be better reached with the Christian message, thus reinforcing the notion that social media is an appropriate place for evangelism.

LifeWay Research (2018) found, from a survey of 1,000 Protestant pastors, that 84% of churches had a Facebook page. However, in another study, the Pew Research Center cited 44% of Facebook users between the ages of 18 and 29 deleted the Facebook app from their mobile phones sometime in the past year to engage with content on other platforms (Perrin, 2018). Unfortunately, LifeWay Research's survey showed that few churches used platforms other than Facebook. For example, only 13% used Instagram. Further, simply having a social media page does not guarantee that it is effective.

This research addresses this problem in two ways. First, it seeks to identify which social media platforms are currently most used among youth and young adults. And second, it seeks to identify what type of content this demographic prefers to see. In doing so, this research aims to help reach youth with the gospel by encouraging churches to bring this message to them in the places where they spend their time, and in the formats they enjoy.

Research Questions

A review of the literature concerning religion and new media suggests that religious organizations have not successfully harnessed the capacity of social media as a tool for evangelism, despite the growing need to invest in ministry across digital platforms. This research aims to answer the question of how SDA social media pages can utilize their platforms to engage more effectively with their audiences in order to build stronger digital spiritual communities that attract youth to the gospel. The primary question for this research is "How can SDA churches, media organizations, and individuals more effectively utilize social media as a tool for evangelism among youth and young adults?" More specifically, this research will explore the questions of 1) Which social media platforms do they prefer? and 2) What type of content do they prefer?

From its founding, the Adventist movement began utilizing the communication resources available for evangelism. The Christian church has been at the cutting edge of communication technology throughout history. To fulfill the Great Commission, churches must continue to stay up to date. As young people continue to communicate using social media, churches must find ways to approach this audience with content that appeals to their demographic. This study examines the most effective way to fulfill the potential of social media so that churches' social media content resonates with the younger audiences whom they are trying to reach and assimilate.

Methods

This research consisted of a quantitative survey administered through Google Forms, collecting data from 375 high school- and college-age students to seek answers to the questions: 1) Which social media platforms do youth prefer? and 2) Which formats of content do youth prefer? The researcher also included three open-ended questions to gain deeper insight into survey responses. Additionally, the researcher conducted an email interview with the owner of a Christian-themed Instagram page with a following of 120,000 (as of September 19, 2021).

Assumptions and Limitations

This research was limited to schools in the United States but not limited to U.S. citizens, as international students studying in the U.S. were included in the sample. The findings from this research should not be generalized as true for all youth. Social media may not be an effective platform for evangelism in some contexts if it is not a prevalent communication channel among youth due to limited internet access or other factors.

This research is also limited in its definition of "youth" as 15- to 24-year-olds, the assumed age of high school and college students. This research also assumed that participants answered all survey questions as accurately as possible. This research was also limited in its control of the participating sample. The researcher reached the sample by sending recruitment emails to 102 SDA high schools and eight SDA colleges across the U.S. From this group, nine high schools and three colleges proceeded to disseminate the survey among its students. The researcher also shared a link to the survey on a personal website and personal social media accounts, encouraging snowball sampling from there.

Finally, this research is limited because social media trends are ever-evolving. What was popular in April of 2021, when the survey closed, will likely not withstand the test of time. So, similar surveys must be administered periodically so that communicators remain up-to-date with what their audience is looking for. In addition, future research could also study the use of social media among people under the age of 15 and over the age of 24. Further research could also explore similar social media use trends in other countries and in other Christian denominations.

Findings

The survey was divided into four sections: demographics, levels of religious interest/affiliation, general social media use, and the intersection of religion and social media.

Demographics. The quantitative survey collected 375 responses. Forty-two percent of respondents were aged 15 to 17, and 52% of respondents were aged 18 to 24. One error in the survey design was corrected partway through the data collection. The first four questions of the survey were intended to serve as filtering questions and were designated to send respondents outside of the target demographic to the end of the survey. However, by not creating a new section after each filtering question, 21 respondents (6%) managed to complete the entire survey although they were under the age of 15 or over 24; their responses were included throughout the study.

All respondents reported that they currently live, work, or study in the U.S. Responses were female-dominated: 65% identified as female, 33% identified as male, and 2% preferred not to answer.

Religiosity. At the beginning of the survey, respondents were asked to report their familiarity with the SDA church on a scale of one to seven, one being labeled as "never heard of it," and seven being "very familiar." The mean of the responses averaged 6.67 (standard deviation = .84).

Perceived Impact. When asked to agree or disagree with the statement, "The religious media I consume strongly impacts my faith," on a scale of one to seven, (one = strongly disagree, and seven = strongly agree) responses were scattered. The mean averaged 4.13 (standard deviation = 1.67). This would suggest that many believe their media consumption does impact their faith, but not strongly. This is interesting to note since, whether or not it is accurate, the perception among youth is that their religious media consumption does not strongly impact their faith. So, there is the possibility that even if Christian creatives share appealing content on the appropriate platforms, social media may still not be an effective tool for evangelism.

Preferred Media Types. The most popular platform for religious media consumption was music; 75% selected this option. Traditional presentations and sermons were the second most popular platform, as 61% selected this option. Books and audiobooks came in third with 51%, and social media came in fourth with 37%. However, only 23% reported using social media as a source of spiritual inspiration.

Preferred Social Media Platforms. Instagram was the most popular platform, as 47% answered that they spent more time there than on other social media platforms. TikTok was the second most popular as 20% selected it as their most-used platform, and YouTube was third with 16%. According to the survey, 73% do not regularly use Twitter and 70% do not regularly use Facebook.

Format. For this research, format refers to the way the information is shared (photo, video, text, etc.). The most preferred formats were highly visual—short videos (80%) and photos (79%). However, responses indicated that respondents disliked blocks of text, defined as three sentences or longer, and videos longer than three minutes.

Content. For this research, content refers to the specific type of information that is shared in a particular format. Seventy-seven percent answered that memes/comics (generally photo or video format) were the most popular type of content. To explore this result further, an email interview was held with the owner of the Instagram account @ChristiansWhoCurseSometimes (CWCS). While striving to maintain anonymity, the CWCS owner explained that he launched this account to harness the power of humor. While dedicating the profile timeline to memes to which Christians can relate, he explores deep, insightful topics on Instagram Stories which expire after 24 hours. With a following of 120,000, CWCS has an impressive reach and has successfully brought together a community through memes that resonate with many Christians. Having found common ground that connects them, he asks inspiring, thought-provoking questions that encourage independent Bible study and receives testimonies via direct messages. Sharing those testimonies anonymously on Instagram Stories has proven to be a powerful tool for helping people learn from each other and feel heard. He says the mission of the CWCS page is "for Christians to have a safe, nonjudgmental space to support others, but also feel excited to ask questions and grow their faith on topics most churches don't talk about." He says, "Social media can make our faith deeper and stronger than ever when we talk and share with others."

Quotes, facts, and infographics (text format) were the second most popular type of content (59%). This may seem like an unusual result. However, it lends itself well to evangelistic content. Designing a brief message as a quote, fact, or infographic may help to catch the eyes of young adults who would otherwise overlook written blocks of text.

Perceived Effectiveness. When asked how strongly they agreed or disagreed with the statement, "Social media is an effective platform for evangelizing," on a scale of one to seven (one = strongly disagree, seven = strongly agree), the mean of the respondents' answers averaged 5.18 (standard deviation = 1.49), suggesting that most agreed that social media is effective for evangelism.

Reasons Social Media is an Effective Platform for Evangelizing.

A follow-up question to the previous one allowed respondents to submit open-ended explanations of why they believe social media is or is not an effective platform for evangelizing. Those who answered that it is an effective platform pointed out that many people use social media, specifically youth, and that it is an efficient method for reaching people from all over the world with diverse backgrounds and perspectives.

One respondent wrote, "Christians on IG [Instagram] have become very popular because of their vulnerability and transparency and a lot of people appreciate that because they are relatable. Social media gives people a chance to connect with other Christians around the world or from different states that, without social media, they may have not had the chance to. It's a great opportunity to find and relate to other Christians and share the gospel with a bigger audience!"

They also pointed out that social media is accessible, free, fast, convenient, and posts are easy to reshare. They observed that it is a safe way to evangelize when people are encouraged to socially distance themselves due to COVID-19, and they appreciate that consumers can avoid confrontations since they can simply unfollow an account or scroll past a post. "Through social media, people can freely browse whatever material they wish or simply scroll past," explained one respondent. "Since, on social media, you aren't forced to watch or listen to something, I feel like people would be more receptive to religious topics. Look at TikTok. There are all sorts of religious videos and I've seen many non-Christians express interest or have genuine inquiries through their comments."

Many respondents personally testified that social media had positively impacted their spiritual lives. One respondent wrote, "Social media, specifically TikTok, has brought me closer to God and has inspired me to read my Bible more often, while still respecting my beliefs and not imposing one specific viewpoint on me." Another wrote, "Something as simple as an inspirational spiritual quote or a Bible verse on Instagram that I see can help me get through the day."

Reasons Social Media is Not an Effective Platform for Evangelizing.
Those who believe social media is not an effective platform for evangelizing expressed concerns that social media, as a whole, is too distracting and shallow of a platform for discussing religious topics; and that since technical algorithms seek to provide people with content that aligns with their existing interests, it would be difficult to reach people who do not already consume religious content. They also suggest that social media is too secular of a platform and that people will become defensive if they see religious content in a place where they were not planning to.

"Social media is the last place my friends and I would go to learn about religious matters or grow spiritually," wrote one respondent. Another respondent wrote, "Social media isn't a good platform for evangelism because people normally get on social media to pass extra time. People aren't going to pay attention unless it is shown in a creative way." Some pointed out that poorly designed content reflects badly on Christianity in general, and that much of the content they have seen is "cheesy," or "forced." Others suggest that when religious content is portrayed on social media it is impersonal and individuals who openly share about their religion may make an impact, but that organizational accounts that do not have a "face" associated with them do not. "People are not looking for a sermon, they're looking for someone just like them," said one respondent.

Others expressed concern that it is difficult to explain religious concepts in a short amount of time and that attempts to do so may misrepresent God and mislead people. Some shared their frustration with social media content that portrays a "holier-than-thou" attitude. Still, others observed that religious content may "conform to worldly expectations" and lose its potency as a form of evangelism in its effort to attract attention.

Finally, some who answered in the middle of the scale proposed that social media is an effective tool for evangelism in the sense that it is a good place to start building relationships. These relationships can then grow into face-to-face conversations, which they maintain are the most effective forms of evangelism. One respondent explained, "I believe the best evangelical opportunities come with intimate conversations between a few people, and that effect can't be accomplished with a post directed at thousands."

Current Exposure to Religious Content on Social Media. When asked how often they saw religious content on social media, only 30% of respondents answered "often" or "always." This suggests that the majority is not regularly exposed to religious content on social media. Further, when asked how often they themselves post or reshare religious social media content, 70% of the responses were "occasionally," or "never."

When asked to rate, on a scale of one to seven, how appealing (one being unappealing and seven being very appealing) the SDA-affiliated social media content they had seen was, the mean of the responses was 3.61 (standard deviation = 1.50). Further, when asked how well Seventh-day Adventists have utilized social media as a tool for evangelism overall, on a scale from one (very poorly) to seven (very well), the mean was 3.37 (standard deviation = 1.33).

Requested Topics to Address on Social Media. One open-ended qualitative question asked what religious topics respondents would like to see social media content creators address. Analysis of these responses yielded eight themes: theology, social issues, taboo topics, relationships, personal testimonies, everyday life, spiritual growth, and service. For an extensive list of the suggested topics in each of these categories, see Appendix A.

One respondent wrote, "I think that we need to start talking about harder topics even if we don't know all of the answers. ...The conversation tends to be more about 'saving' teenagers instead of empowering them to lead their peers to Jesus. ...There are systemic failures in our [the SDA] Church. When teenagers see the world making more progress concerning equality and having the hard conversations that our church, in general, is not having, it looks like we are saying that these things are okay and that nothing can change. Discussions with multiple points of view will not only talk about things that are interesting to teens but will also show them that we can live in harmony even if we disagree."

Suggestions for Improvement. Another open-ended qualitative question requested feedback on how Seventh-day Adventists can better utilize social media as a tool for evangelism. Most responses fell into one of three categories: content, activity, or attitude. For an extensive list of the feedback given under each of these categories, see Appendix B. "Seventh-day Adventists should be encouraged to share more religious topics on social media, and I think that having a large variety of SDA bloggers, YouTubers, content creators, etc. can help draw many more people to the faith," wrote one respondent. "I also think that the SDA church should put a bigger emphasis on witnessing/evangelism in general, and what easier place to start than one's social media accounts." Responses also encouraged content creators to glean inspiration from the Instagram accounts @HerTrueWorth, @Forerunner777, @HumansOfAdventism, and @TryTheWay.

Finally, according to this survey, nearly three out of four youth (74%) between the ages of 15 and 24 spend at least one hour on social media each day. Further, only 23% currently use social media for spiritual inspiration, 62% would like to see more religious content on social media, and 74% say that seeing more appealing religious social media content would improve their view of the Church. All of these statistics suggest that there is a compelling opportunity for churches, media organizations, and digital missionaries to utilize social media as a tool for evangelism. This may require training and educating church leaders who are willing to invest in learning the trends or encouraging members to take advantage of their personal accounts as platforms for witnessing.

The data collected from this survey indicate that, currently, evangelistic social media content will be most effective if it is delivered through Instagram, TikTok, and YouTube. When deciding what type of content to post, creatives should consider sharing memes, quotes, facts, and infographics in the formats of short videos and photos. And when selecting what topics to cover, creators should reference the list of suggestions gathered, through this survey, directly from the target audience (Appendix A).

Youth have questions and crave conversations that surround the real issues they are facing. By taking all of these factors, as well as direct suggestions for improvement, into consideration, Christian social media managers will better understand their audiences, and be better equipped to create content that appeals to youth and young adults.

Conclusion

As technology continues to develop, the churches must continue to adapt in order to strategically place the gospel where people will find and hear it. As social media becomes an increasingly popular channel for connecting with and communicating to mass audiences of a younger demographic, it seems also to be an ideal platform for evangelizing to the rising generation of future church leaders.

This research is particularly timely due to the COVID-19 pandemic requiring churches to be exceptionally creative and resourceful in their communication methods during a time when people are advised to limit face-to-face interaction. Further, on a larger scale, the implications of this study may help to spread the gospel, via social media, more quickly and more widely in order to expedite the second coming of Christ.

Returning to the framework for this research, the uses and gratifications theory of media choice states that people actively pursue the media that will satisfy their needs. To reach young people effectively with evangelistic social media content, creators need to deliberately cater content to meet their audience's needs. If Christians can curate appealing content, perhaps it will attract the eyes of youth on social media, and the hopeful message of the gospel will fulfill the spiritual needs of sinful, broken human lives seeking answers and truth during their young, developing years.

References

Carlson, J. R., & Zmud, R. W. (1999). Channel expansion theory and the experiential nature of media richness perceptions. *Academy of Management Journal, 42*(2), 153–170.

Daft, R. L., & Lengel, R. H. (1984). Information richness: A new approach to managerial behavior and organizational design. *Research in Organizational Behavior, 6*, 191–233.

Dunaetz, D. R. (2019). Evangelism, social media, and the mum effect. *Evangelical Review of Theology, 43*(2), 138–151.

Katz, E., Blumler, J. G., & Gurevitch, M. (1973). Uses and gratifications research. *Public Opinion Quarterly, 37*(4), 509-523.

LifeWay Research. (2018). *Most churches offer wi-fi but skip Twitter.* https://lifewayresearch.com/2018/01/09/most-churches-offer-free-wi-fi-but-skip-twitter/

McChesney, A. (2016). U.S. Adventists older than new Pew study suggests. *Adventist Review.* https://www.adventistreview.org/church-news/story4221-us-adventists-older than-new-pew-study-suggests

Nduka, E. L., & McGuire, J. (2017). The effective use of new media in disseminating evangelical messages among Catholic college students. *Journal of Media & Religion, 16*(3), 93–103.

North American Division. (2018). Global church member survey. *Adventist Research.* https://www.adventistresearch.info/wp-content/uploads/2017-2018-GCMS-NAD-final-public-report-pages.pdf

Perrin, A. (2020). *Americans are changing their relationship with Facebook.* Pew Research. https://www.pewresearch.org/fact-tank/2018/09/05/americans-are-changing-their-relationship-with-facebook/

Ratcliff, A. J., McCarty, J., & Ritter, M. (2017). Religion and new media: A uses and gratifications approach. Journal of Media and Religion, 16(1), 15–26.

Reddy, M. M. (2019). Organisational communication: Types of communication used by the Seventh-Day Adventist Church in spreading Christianity. *Gender & Behaviour*, 17(1), 12674–12695.

Richter, F. (2018, October 9*). Infographic: Teens' Social Media Usage Is Drastically Increasing*. Statista. https://www.statista.com/chart/15720/frequency-of-teenagers-social-media-use/

Strate, L. (2017). Understanding the message of Understanding Media. *Atlantic Journal of Communication, 25*(4), 244–254.

Tudor, M. A., & Herteliu, A. M. (2016). The usages of Internet and new media by the Romanian Seventh-day Adventist clergy. *Journal for the Study of Religions & Ideologies, 15*(45), 207–233.

Appendix A

Religious Topics SDA Youth Would Like to See Addressed on Social Media

Theology

- Clarifying myths of out-of-context verses
- Clarifying myths/attacks on Ellen White
- Historicity of the Bible
- SDA-unique doctrines explained
- Reconciliation of Old Testament and New Testament God
- Satan/how the Devil works
- Second Coming/Last Day events/Daniel and Revelation
- What it means to keep the Sabbath/what's allowed and not allowed
- Are other denominations going to heaven?

Social Issues

- Homosexuality and the LGBTQIA+ community
- Intersectionality/racism and racial diversity
- Gender roles/sexism/misogyny (and women's ordination)
- Social justice
- Generational gap in Church leadership
- Interpersonal relations with other faiths, religions, etc., including non-religious people and atheists. Generally, how to coexist with others without feeling attacked when someone doesn't believe the way you do. How to respect others who do not believe in/do not practice your faith.

Taboo Topics

- Physical, sexual, and emotional abuse
- Anxiety & depression
- Sex
- Drugs
- Alcohol
- Bullying
- Cursing
- Pornography
- Drums/rhythm in music
- Jewelry and tattoos
- Abortion
- Meat consumption

Relationships

- Parenting
- Finding wholesome friends

- Singleness
- Dating
- Marriage
- Divorce

Testimonies

- Personal stories of God's work in someone's life
- Missionary miracles
- Outreach successes

Everyday Life

- Navigating a secular workplace as an Adventist
- Hope during current events in light of God's promises
- School/value of education
- Intersection of career and calling
- How to be cheerful and enjoy life
- Diet and health message

Personal Spiritual Growth

- How to continue growing your relationship with God when you have a pretty good relationship with Him. How do you "fall in love" with God? How do you not get bored with God and Church? How do you "spice up" your devotion time? What are a lot of different ways you could do devotions?
- Salvation/God's personal love and grace, accepting others
- Ways to build a relationship with God other than church and Bible study
- How to start a relationship with God
- How to approach those in sin without judgment
- Prayer life/how to pray
- How to study the Bible
- Encouraging verses/quotes/daily reminders
- Christlike character/Fruits of the Spirit/not being "of the world"
- Navigating grief
- Forgiveness
- Spiritual stagnation
- Finding/feeling peace
- Avoiding temptation

Service

- How youth can get involved
- Media projects
- How to witness
- Outreach ideas
- How individuals can use social media as a tool for evangelism

Appendix B

Suggestions for How Seventh-day Adventists Can Better Utilize Social Media as a Tool for Evangelism

Content

- Discuss "relevant" topics (see suggestions in Appendix A)
- More interactive content/trivia/Q&A sessions
- Make content aesthetically pleasing, give the account a theme and a professional look because youth are more likely to reshare content that is aesthetically appealing
- Give posts better titles
- Write longer captions and add value beyond just quoting a Bible verse
- Share multiple perspectives on a topic
- Use humor/memes
- Videos (music videos, short videos, TikToks, by teens for teens, daily devotionals)
- Encourage individuals to be influencers for Christ/digital discipleship/individual contributions: show us the books used for devotionals, meals, lifestyle
- Post more outings with the church to bring in people from the community
- Host events on social media
- Build on previous posts to provide long-term content in small chunks that encourage people to watch for future posts

Activity

- Have youth create the content
- Interact more consistently with followers
- Encourage youth pastors to interact on social media
- Pay for promotion/advertising/sponsorship
- Be consistent and persistent
- Just put out more content
- Invest in social media managers who are informed about the current trends

Attitude

- Make it a safe place for anyone to come to (this may include turning off comments to prevent the audience from engaging in hostile arguments)
- See teenage phone use as an opportunity for evangelism, not an addiction
- Be raw, have emotion, and have passion

About the Author

Trisney Janine Bocala-Wiedemann received her bachelor's degree in mass communication–advertising from Southern Adventist University's School of Journalism and Communication. She currently works in public relations with Matter Communications.

GREAT COMMISSION
RESEARCH JOURNAL
2022, Vol. 14(1) 35-49

An Examination of Three Models of Missional Communities for Sharing the Gospel with Muslims in the United States

Mike Urton
Evangelical Free Church of America

Abstract

Missional communities are small groups within a local church that serve those outside the church with the aim of sharing the gospel, perhaps even providing them the possibility of joining the group. Missional communities have been used effectively by local churches in reaching the surrounding community or a specific group of people. This article examines three different models of missional communities, discussing the strengths and challenges associated with each one. Based on these observations, along with observations on the evangelical Christian and Muslim communities in the United States, three recommendations are presented for helping missional communities effectively share the gospel with a local Muslim community.

Three Models of Missional Communities

Justin Smith offers a concise definition of a missional community as "an expression of the church that seeks to serve the communities around them" (Smith, 2013, p.190). While this definition can be applied to both whole congregations as well as smaller groups within a congregation, for our purposes we will be focusing on missional communities as small groups within a local church who serve those outside the church with the aim of sharing the gospel with them or having them join the group.

To gain a better understanding of missional communities, we will examine the view of three authors and practitioners: Scott Boren (2010), Mike Breen (2013), and Reggie McNeal (2011). We will examine how these authors define missional communities, what they believe the proper size to be, and how they should be structured.

Scott Boren

Scott Boren (2010) describes missional communities as small groups of people who are "committed to live in community with one another in everyday life, and [who have] a call to minister together outside of official meetings" (p.17). These are groups that "experience community for the sake of participating in God's redemption of creation" (2010, p.23).

Boren sharpens this definition by identifying three topics that shape missional communities. First, is the realization that Western Christians live in a time where they need to view themselves as missionaries in their own countries. Second, Christians need to ask "what it means to be the church and how the people of God should be a sign, witness, and foretaste of God's dream for the world" (Boren, 2010, p. 25). Third, they need to discuss the broad implications of the gospel and how God is at work in the world, enabling them to discern how God's Spirit is at work and to "see how small groups can be more than a support system for church as we know it or as a method for resurrecting a dying church system" (Boren, 2010, p.25). Such groups will help God's people to understand how to join God in what he is already doing by, for example, helping with refugee resettlement or serving the surrounding community alongside local religious leaders.

This last point emphasizes why it is important for those participating in a missional community to understand how their group fits into "the specific location and culture of a neighborhood" (Boren 2010, p.64). Boren argues that this is how foreign missionaries conduct their ministry when they enter a new culture, seeking to discover how to best live out their ministry calling in that context. They begin by listening to the local people's concerns and praying for them; through this, "the Good News of Jesus rises up and becomes real in specific situations" (Boren, 2010, p.131). Since Western Christians need to view themselves as missionaries to their own culture, they must also practice how to contextualize their ministry in similar ways. Boren urges that this best happens in a community. It is not simply for "individuals who feel called to 'reach people for Christ'" (Boren, 2010, p.132).

For a missional community to be successful, it must have a presence in a neighborhood and its members must interact with people in such a way that they know the members of the missional community care for them. Christians should follow Jesus' example of ministering locally in a specific place (Boren, 2010). Serving a specific neighborhood will help those in the missional community get to know the people in the community on a personal level, enabling them to share the gospel in a way that feels authentic. Such a presence will cause the missional community to be seen "as people who live in this world and as people who have a God who can do something about what is going on in this world" (Boren, 2010, p.135).

Boren's vision for a missional community is that its members will frequently interact with their neighbors by sharing their joys and struggles in life so that their neighbors will grow to trust them. This will allow non-Christian neighbors to see how the gospel changes lives and gives "them access to not only the God who can change their lives but also a community that can embrace them and walk with them through their life situations" (Boren, 2010, p.161). In these missional communities, both believers and non-believers are invited by the group to take steps towards Jesus and to embrace him and his kingdom.

Mike Breen

Central to Mike Breen's (2013) definition of a missional community is the New Testament word *oikos*, the Greek word for "household." In the New Testament context, households were "essentially extended families who functioned together with a common purpose" and that "discipleship and mission always centered around and flourished in the oikos" (Breen, 2013, loc. 106). His definition of a missional community is an oikos formed by Christians, "an extended family on mission where everyone contributes and everyone is supported" (Breen, 2013, loc. 119).

Breen believes that there are four foundational principles for missional communities. First, they are to be communities for the purpose of disciple making. He defines a disciple as someone who learns to trust and follow Jesus in every area of life, grows in Christlike character, and becomes more competent in ministry (Breen 2013, loc. 253). In a missional community, leaders intentionally train disciples who will multiply themselves by training more disciples. Breen states "we are called to participate in the advance of the Kingdom of God by making disciples who become leaders and multiply to make more disciples" (Breen, 2013, loc. 329-341).

Breen's second foundational principle is that missional communities are to be communities focused on sharing the good news. The group is to embody and proclaim the gospel. Here the missional community is to "tell the whole story of the good news of Jesus Christ" in both words and actions (Breen, 2013, loc. 369).

The third principle flows out of the second: The missional community is directed towards those considered to be Persons of Peace. In Luke 10:1-16, the Person of Peace was someone who welcomed Jesus' disciples "into his or her home, was open to the message they were bringing, and served them" (Breen,

2013, loc. 516). Just as the disciples were to seek out this type of person who was open to them and their message, so should Christians today who are trying to reach a particular neighborhood or relational network, such as another religious community. Identifying people who may be Persons of Peace is important because "they are people in whom God has already been working, preparing their hearts for the good news of Jesus" (Breen, 2013, loc. 526).

Breen's (2013) fourth principle is that missional communities are to cultivate both the organized and organic elements of community. These elements include both the organized activities of a missional community as well as the more informal activities and events in life. The organic element could include events like hosting a group for dinner or spontaneous activities like a pick-up basketball game. Breen warns that there are two equal and opposite errors groups can make. "Let us state it as strongly as possible: If your missional community is doing only organized events, it will fail. If your missional community is committed only to the organic 'hanging out' together, it will fail" (Breen, 2013, loc. 631). It is necessary to discover the right balance for each missional community so that "they become places where people experience being an extended family on mission" (Breen, 2013, loc. 619-31).

While Breen's (2013) vision for a missional community has much in common with Boren's (2010), his view of evangelism and discipleship seems to be more intentional than Boren's. Whereas Boren (2010) appears leery of the goal of growth in the missional community, Breen (2013) makes no apology that this is to be the aim of the group. He writes, "Our commission is to compassionately reach out to those around us, invite them to join us in community, share the story of the gospel, make disciples, and gather them into families to follow Jesus together. That's really what starting a missional community is all about" (Breen, 2013, loc. 119). These missional communities are to intentionally and compassionately serve a specific group of people and actively invite them to follow Christ.

Breen (2013) agrees with Boren (2010) that missional communities are to adapt to the specific context in which they are ministering. Yet, Breen (2013) expands the types of audience which can be the focus of missional communities. While Boren (2010) encourages missional communities to impact a specific neighborhood, Breen (2013) adds that they can also impact a network (Breen 2013, loc. 144). So, Breen's (2013) model can be employed to reach out to a specific religious group within the neighborhood, such as the Muslim community, a group often overlooked when Christians think about local outreach.

Reggie McNeal

Soma is a network of missional communities in the Seattle area, described by Reggie McNeal (2011) in *Missional Communities: The Rise of the Post Congregational Church*. Soma defines a missional community as "a committed core of believers (family) who live out the mission together (missionaries) in a specific area or to a particular people group by demonstrating the gospel in tangible forms (servants) and declaring the gospel to others—both those who believe it and those who are being exposed to it (learners)" (McNeal, 2011, loc. 1338).

Members of a Soma missional community must have "a proper grasp of the gospel, along with its implications for a believer's identity in Christ and how the gospel can be lived out in basic life rhythms" (McNeal, 2011, loc. 1346). Thus for Soma, their understanding of the gospel has two elements: theological and missional. The theological side is understanding that the gospel is God's power to save sinners through the redemptive work of Christ. The missional side flows out of the theological as believers grasp the gospel as a story of redemption for the whole world. "This takes place as the disciples of Jesus make other disciples who live out their role as agents of renewal in all areas of culture—the arts, business, politics, families, education—all domains of human activity" (McNeal, 2011, loc. 1361).

Participants in Soma's missional communities have four primary identities: family members, missionaries, servants, and learners. As family members, they care for one another as followers of Christ. As missionaries, they are sent out by God into the world "to live in such a way that people can see and experience what God is truly like" (McNeal, 2011, loc. 1370). As servants, they simply seek to "serve others as a way of life," and as learners, they take "responsibility for [their] own development and that of others" (McNeal, 2011, loc. 1370-78).

Soma's (McNeal, 2011) conception of a missional community is similar to Boren's (2010) and Breen's (2013), especially concerning a missionary emphasis and service to those whom they seek to reach. However, McNeal's Soma communities place a greater emphasis on the theological implications of the gospel for their members. This is to foster believers' growth by developing a "strong identity of being the people of God, not just as a result of doing a bunch of church programming" (McNeal, 2011, loc. 1331).

Size of a Missional Community

There is considerable variation among these authors concerning the size of a missional community. Boren (2010, p. 103) believes that a group should consist of 5-12 people who are willing to share life together and have a sense of belonging. McNeal's (2011, loc. 1448) Soma communities are slightly larger ranging, from 8 to 20, with 12 to 14 members being typical.

Breen (2013) thinks that a missional community needs to be much larger with 20 to 40 people. While he would allow for a group to be 12 to 15, he holds that the 20 to 40 size is ideal. He supports this size stating missional communities need to be "small enough to care but also big enough to dare" (loc. 156). This means the group should be small enough for everyone to be cared for and to contribute, but large enough to carry out the group's mission. The groups should also be large enough that people feel comfortable visiting and observing the group without having to make a commitment.

A final advantage to a missional community with 20 to 40 members is that the group can multiply easily. According to Breen (2013), smaller groups are more intimate, making it more difficult to divide because people do not want to leave the close relationships they have built.

Breen (2013) is critical of the smaller-sized groups suggested by Boren (2010) and the Soma communities for two main reasons. First, a smaller group lacks the semi-autonomous nature of a mid-sized one. This makes it more difficult to add people who just want to visit the group as observers (Breen 2013, loc. 157). Second, a group with fewer than 15 adults usually become inwardly focused. This reduces the multiplying potential of the missional community. Due to these factors, Breen insists that "size does matter in missional communities" (Breen 2013, loc. 156).

Structure of a Missional Community

Scott Boren

Boren's (2010) missional communities are structured around three basic rhythms: Missional Communion, Missional Relating, and Missional Engagement. Missional Communion concerns how people in the group relate to God: worshipping, listening to God through Scripture, praying together, and sharing communion which he calls "the Jesus meal." Boren believes that relating to God "is basic and foundational to anything we do missionally" (2010, p. 70).

Missional Relating concerns how the members of the missional community relate to each other. Appealing to John 13:34-35 where Jesus tells his followers that the world will know that they are his disciples if they love one another, Boren comments "The way we relate to one another is as important to our missional way of being in the world as anything else" (Boren 2010, p. 101). Through this rhythm, the missional community creates a safe atmosphere, resolves conflict, and builds one another up.

Boren (2010) cautions against jumping to the final rhythm, Missional Engagement, without previously developing the first two rhythms. Many people will want to begin with this third rhythm because it is "where the action is" (Boren 2010, p. 131). However, "those who jump into this rhythm without considering how the first two rhythms shape our lives as a people who are distinctively God's soon find that Missional Engagement loses its sustaining power" (Boren 2010, p. 131). Therefore, he encourages those who want to launch a missional community to consider how "the three rhythms reinforce one another for Missional Engagement around us" (Boren 2010, p. 131).

After this warning, he defines Missional Engagement as "doing Missional Communion and Missional Relating before those in the neighborhood" (Boren

2010, p. 134), or practicing the first two rhythms in full view of those in the surrounding community. This is a more natural way to do evangelism than program-based evangelism.

While he mentions several ways to practice Missional Engagement, Boren (2010) emphasizes practicing hospitality. He points out that the word hospitality, in *koine* Greek, simply means the love of strangers. It is through this practice that those in the missional community create space for those who are "different or unknown" (Boren 2010, p. 149).

He highlights three concrete aspects of hospitality. First is the welcome and conversation that others experience in our homes. Second, hospitality revolves around how we eat food and connect spiritually. Third, it is important to refrain from trying to convert someone because hospitality receives people as they are. However, this does not mean that we jettison or hide our beliefs, but we introduce our guests to the gospel while conversing with them (Boren 2010, p. 151-53). In many Muslim cultures, hospitality is a cherished value and can be especially effective when interacting with Muslims.

Mike Breen

Mike Breen outlines five characteristics of a missional community's structure. The first concerns the size of the group already discussed. The second characteristic is the development of a clear vision of their mission. This vision is to be "focused on sharing the good news of Jesus and making disciples among the people of a specific neighborhood or network of relationships" (Breen 2013, loc. 169-181). It is this vision that draws people into the missional community and provides the motivation to keep the group moving.

Lightweight/low-Maintenance is the third characteristic of Breen's missional community model. The emphasis here is on making the group a lifestyle rather than a set of programs or events to run. The goal is to set up sustainable rhythms "by missionally focusing the activities we are already involved in, rather than adding more events and extra commitments to the calendar" (Breen 2013, loc. 194). In other words, it is using the activities that people in the group are already doing for missional purposes.

The leader's accountability to a central church is the fourth characteristic of Breen's (2013) missional community. While the church will have low control over the group, the accountability of the leader will be high. Low control over the group is necessary to ensure that the leader has the freedom to act according to the needs and opportunities that develop. But it is through high accountability to the central church that the leader is equipped and supported to lead the group. This accountability may take the form of a regular meeting with a church leader to review the missional community's vision and activities, with the church leader providing the necessary encouragement and counsel.

The final characteristic of Breen's (2013) missional community is an up/in/out rhythm. Up focuses on community members' relationship with

God. In focuses on the relationships within the community. Out focuses on outreach to the community. The community's vision for mission, along with this threefold rhythm, allows a missional community, to be "an extended family on mission together" (Breen, 2013, loc. 218).

Reggie McNeal

Soma communities are structured around six "cultural rhythms" (McNeal, 2011, loc. 1388). The first is that they are story-formed. This means that these missional communities "Understand, experience, and intersect with God's story and others'" (McNeal, 2011, loc. 1388). Leaders instill this rhythm into the group at the beginning of each year (typically after a break) by going through discipleship material called the Story-Formed Way. This curriculum walks the community through the basics of the Gospel message and the core doctrines of Christianity. It is available online as a free download (https://saturatetheworld.com/resource/story-formed-way/).

Next, these Missional communities take time to listen to God "both 'backward' and 'forward'" (McNeal, 2011, loc. 1402-3). This involves listening to God in Scripture, the 'backward' element, while at the same time listening to the Holy Spirit through prayer for guidance, the 'forward' element.

Celebration of the blessings that God has bestowed is the third rhythm. These are weekly gatherings at both the missional community-level and the larger congregational-level. The larger congregational meetings are what Soma calls Expressions, where a number of groups gather together. The purpose of these gatherings "is to celebrate all that God is doing in and among the people of the missional community" (McNeal, 2011, loc. 1406).

The fourth rhythm is intentionally blessing others. This is focused on the group the missional community has chosen to serve and where they will seek to make disciples of Jesus.

Eating meals with others constitutes the fifth rhythm. Group members are accountable to each other for having meals with those outside the missional community whom they are trying to reach. Related to this is the sixth rhythm of taking "time to rest, play, create, and restore beauty in ways that reflect God to others" (McNeal, 2011, loc. 1421-28). This includes celebrating with those inside and outside the group, as well as looking for "ways to add beauty to their surroundings, whether in beautification projects or art projects in local neighborhoods" (McNeal, 2011, loc. 1429-31).

While all three of these models seek a balance between organization and flexibility, it appears that Boren (2010) emphasizes flexibility the most concerning the structure of missional communities. Both Breen (2013) and the Soma communities (McNeal, 2011) emphasize a more organized structure, providing specific guidelines for a missional community. Those who prefer a little more freedom and flexibility will favor Boren's model, whereas those looking for more structure will gravitate towards Breen and Soma when launching a group.

The Muslim Community in the United States and Christian Attitudes Towards Them

Now that we have discussed the nature of missional communities, we will look at the Muslim community in the United States and Christians' attitudes towards Muslims. This will lead to specific recommendations for how missional communities can influence a local Muslim community with the gospel.

According to the Pew Forum, 3.45 million Muslims call the United States their home (Pew Forum, 2017). This is a diverse group of people including both immigrants from throughout the world and natural-born U.S. citizens. A Pew researcher has projected that "by 2040, Muslims will replace Jews as the nation's second-largest religious group after Christians. And by 2050, the U.S. Muslim population is projected to reach 8.1 million, or 2.1% of the nation's total population — nearly twice the share of today" (Mohamed, 2018).

Yet reports of evangelical Christian attitudes towards Muslims in the U.S., such as "Most White Evangelicals Don't Think Muslims Belong in America" (Shellnut, 2017), paint a discouraging picture. A LifeWay Research study of evangelical pastors' attitudes towards Islam indicated that half the respondents characterized Islam as spiritually evil, dangerous, and promoting violence (Green 2015). For many evangelicals, mistrust of Muslims is high even before any relationship begins.

If we are going to move past these obstacles to better share the gospel with Muslims, then we need to think deeply about our view of other religions and Islam more specifically. Harold Netland (2001) provides evangelicals with two conditions for formulating a theology of other religions. First, it must be based on Scripture and consistent with historic, orthodox Christianity. Second, it must be accurate in its description of other religious traditions (Netland, 2001, p. 313). He argues that adherents of other religions are created in God's image and have access to general revelation. Thus these religious others will know some truth about God and do some things that are morally commendable (Rom. 1-2). Yet because of human sinfulness (Matt. 23:1-36) and the influence of Satan and his demons (2 Cor. 4:4), adherents of other religions cannot know the one true God through practicing their faith, but only through God's self-revelation in Scripture (Netland, 2001, p. 331-36).

Encouraging Christians to live faithfully in the multi-faith context of North America, Ed Stetzer offers four principles. The first is to let each religion speak for itself. This is similar to Netland's concern for accurate descriptions of others' belief systems. It is important for Christians to listen to adherents of other faiths in order to "learn what people actually believe" (Stetzer, 2018, p. 11).

Second, Stetzer (2018) instructs Christians to talk with and about individuals without assuming that religions are monolithic belief systems. This will help them to avoid stereotyping everyone of a particular religion based on the actions of a few (Stetzer, 2018, p. 11).

Third, Christians should respect the beliefs of people of other religions without distorting them, just as we would want them to respect and accurately describe Christian beliefs. Stetzer comments, "It is simply unfair and unchristian to sit by and allow or actively take part in lying about those of another religion" (2018, p. 13).

Finally, people must be granted the freedom to make their own decisions concerning what they believe. Here Christians must realize that they cannot compel others to believe a certain way and that others have the right to choose their own path regardless of the consequences. This attitude is seen in Jesus when he forbade his disciples to use force after they were rejected in a Samaritan village (Luke 9:54-55; Stetzer, 2018, p. 15).

Amit Bhatia (2015) agrees with Netland's criteria and would find much in common with Stetzer's four commitments as he focuses specifically on Islam. He suggests that Islam's focus on monotheism is something that evangelicals can commend, especially its emphasis on submission to God and morality. In line with Stetzer's admonition to respect the beliefs of others, Bhatia cautions against speaking disrespectfully of the Qur'an and Muhammad due to the high reverence Muslims have for them. Similar to Netland's idea that other religions contain some truth, Bhatia encourages evangelicals to affirm truths in Islam that agree with the Bible and to use them as "connecting points to engage Muslims" (Bhatia, 2015, p. 132). Finally, he advises evangelicals to be informed of the political issues in the Muslim world, especially discussions concerning violence and terrorism, paying attention to the complexity of these issues (Bhatia, 2015, p. 132-34).

Bhatia (2015) also offers some helpful suggestions as to how Christians should approach Muslims. He argues that Christians should be aware of their own biases due to the violence committed by Islamic radicals, as well as recognize that not all Muslims support such violence. He also holds that Christians should develop a healthy appreciation for Islamic culture and treat Muslims by the Golden Rule as we would want to be treated (Bhatia, 2015, p. 134). The importance of the Golden Rule is affirmed by Stetzer and is also emphasized by David Gustafson, Chair of Mission and Evangelism at Trinity Evangelical Divinity School. He writes, "The Golden Rule provides clarity for how we should treat religious others, including how we engage in witness, share the gospel, and practice Christian apologetics" (Gustafson, 2019, p. 170).

By anchoring themselves in Scripture and historic, orthodox Christian theology, as Netland (2001) encourages, Christians can engage members of other religions with confidence. Stetzer's (2018) four principles provide practical guidelines for navigating relationships with those from a different religious background. Bhatia (2015) shows how to interact with Muslims specifically and even how to start conversations about religion. Using the Golden Rule as a guide, we can pursue relationships with Muslims, communicating the compassion of Christ.

Interacting with Muslims in North America through Missional Communities

Since we have addressed Christians' attitudes towards Muslims and how they should interact with them, we will now address how Christians in a missional community can reach out to and serve Muslims near them.

Richard Kronk and colleagues (2017), in conjunction with Tyndale Intercultural Ministry (TIM) Center at Tyndale University College and Seminary in Toronto, Canada, conducted a study of Christians who minister among Muslims in North America and found that one of the top three reasons for Muslims coming to Christ was an experience with a local evangelical church. Missional communities, as part of local congregations, can certainly expect to play a significant role in seeing Muslims become disciples of Christ. Developing a clear mission vision, practicing hospitality, and serving the Muslim community will enable a missional community to effectively share the gospel with Muslims in the United States.

A Clear Mission Vision

A missional community focusing on a particular group of people needs a clear mission vision (Breen, 2013). Clarity of vision will assist the missional community to stay focused on interacting with Muslims and can be used to attract others in the church who also have a desire to reach Muslims.

Some people in a local church will encounter Muslims at work and possibly in their neighborhood, but only about 22% of U.S. evangelicals interact frequently with Muslims (Foundation for Ethnic Understanding 2019) and less than half that number would say they have a close friend who is Muslim (Mogahed and Mahmood 2019, p. 21). Similarly, it is likely many Muslims do not have close friends outside of their own community. Moreover, Christians may have fears to overcome or a lack of knowledge of how to reach out to them. Therefore, a local Muslim community is what Breen (2013) would call "a 'crevice' of society where a gospel presence is lacking." He encourages Christians to specifically focus on such communities so that the principal growth of the missional community will come from those who have had the least exposure to the Gospel.

Members of a missional community with a focus on reaching Muslims need training on effectively living out the gospel in a local Muslim community (Urton, 2021). This will require a curriculum like *Journey to Jesus: Building Christ-centered Friendships with Muslims* (Oksnevad and Urton, 2014) or *Bridges: Christians Connecting with Muslims* (Masri, 2008) to encourage interacting with Muslims with confidence. Soma's Story-Formed Way material would also be valuable because it teaches Christians how to share the entire narrative of Scripture with their Muslim friends. The vast majority of Muslims do not have an understanding of Scripture as the story of God's redemption, so this is an effective way of communicating many aspects of the gospel.

Hospitality

Hospitality will prove valuable for members of a missional community as they develop relationships with Muslims. In most Muslim cultures hospitality is highly valued. Thabiti Anyabwile writes, "Muslims, who typically practice hospitality on a regular basis, value such actions by others. When we show hospitality, we welcome them into our lives" (Anyabwile, 2010, p. 123).

While it is important that Christians open their homes to Muslims, sharing their faith and lives with them, it is equally important that Christians receive the hospitality that Muslims extend to them. In doing so, Christians demonstrate their appreciation of Islamic culture, their generosity and hospitality, and thereby honor their Muslim neighbors (Bhatia, 2015).

Joshua Jipp (2017), associate professor of New Testament at Trinity Evangelical Divinity School, also argues that Christians need to receive the hospitality of people of other religions, based on the example of the apostle Paul where he, along with the sailors shipwrecked with him, received it from the Maltese in Acts 28. When befriending Muslims, this can be done by accepting an invitation to an *Iftar* (the breaking of the fast dinner during Ramadan) or any other offer of hospitality extended by a Muslim host. Jipp hopes that in both giving and receiving hospitality from others, Christians will:

> engage in personal encounters where they can both share their own stories and listen to the stories and experiences of non-Christian neighbors. This hospitable openness can perhaps best take place in one another's homes where hospitable interaction with the religious other can entail offering clear and sensitive explanations of one's own faith commitments and religious practices (2017, p. 115).

Both Boren (2010) and Jipp (2017) believe that practicing hospitality should lead to conversations where Christians can both share their faith and learn about the faith of others. Certainly, listening to and learning from Muslim neighbors is needed when practicing hospitality, but it is also important for believers to be intentional about introducing their faith to Muslims. Unlike many Westerners, Muslims respect a deep commitment to religion and find it refreshing when they see it, especially when living in a secular culture. As one Muslim friend stated after spending an evening in our home, "I didn't know there were people like you here in America." He had never met Christians who took their faith seriously and verbalized it.

Expressing one's faith does not need to take the form of a gospel presentation with an invitation to receive Christ, but rather it can be communicated in gracious ways that fit with the flow of the time together. For example, many Muslims, both first and second generation, do not know much about Christian holidays. They are surrounded by holiday décor every Easter and Christmas but have no idea what the symbols mean. Yet many are curious about their meaning, seeing them displayed so prominently every holiday season. Thus, explaining the meaning of an Advent calendar, the significance of biblically themed ornaments, or the relationship between Passover and Easter can introduce them to elements of the Christian faith and potentially spark deeper conversations about the gospel.

All these aspects of hospitality can be included in the rhythm of a missional community by inviting Muslim guests to a potluck or picnic. As Anyabwile observes "Maybe the best way for us Christians to build friendships with Muslim neighbors the Lord has brought to our doorsteps is to host them in our homes. We may reach the world for Christ by simply reaching across our picket fences or crossing the street and then inviting them into our dining and family rooms" (2010, p. 124).

Community Service Projects

Lesslie Newbigin believed that Christians should be "eager to cooperate with people of all faiths and ideologies in all projects which are in line with the Christian's understanding of God's purpose in history" (1989, loc. 3390). In other words, Christians should be willing to work with people of other faiths on issues and projects that line up with God's purposes for the community. This is similar to Soma's rhythm of restoring beauty in a way that reflects God to others (McNeal 2011, loc. 1429-31). Therefore, believers involved in a missional community can look for ways to organize and participate in joint-service projects alongside their Muslim friends.

A joint Muslim-Christian service effort should ask Boren's (2010) questions for determining the particular needs of a community and deciding where to serve. These questions include asking about the community's greatest assets, what people like about living or working in the community, what needs to change in the community, and the greatest need in the community (Boren 2010, p. 148-49). This could be done in conjunction with the leadership of a local mosque to encourage participation in and ownership of a joint project.

Asking such questions can uncover needs such as school children requiring tutors, elderly people hoping for yard work, or food banks lacking labor. Discussing needs can lead to projects such as painting a run-down building or planting trees in a local park. Given the Muslim values of service and community improvement, these are all projects that Christians and Muslims could work on together.

During these service projects, members of the missional community can look for opportunities to share bits of information about who Christ is and what he has done in their lives. Newbigin (1989) believed that this is where true dialogue begins as we serve with others while discussing the real issues of a community. He writes "the essential contribution of the Christian to the dialogue will simply be the telling of the story, the story of Jesus, the story of the Bible" (Newbigin, 1989, loc. 3415).

Conclusion

A missional community with a clear vision to reach Muslims can employ these suggestions from the inception of the group. Yet they must also realize that the journey ahead will be a long and challenging one. Gustafson offers this exhortation when working with people of other religions, "We must start where religiously diverse people are in their understandings of God, the Bible, and the gospel of Jesus Christ. This requires a long journey for some people to come to faith in Jesus Christ. We must walk patiently with them step-by-step, taking time to explain the gospel in words and to demonstrate its truth in deeds" (Gustafson, 2019, p. 151). This is especially true with members of a local Muslim community. Perhaps a focused and committed missional community can eventually, after years of service, see their Muslim neighbors, created in God's image, become disciples of the Lord Jesus Christ. Hopefully, these disciples, with a similar focus and support structure, can be used by God to start a movement within their own people by reproducing their own missional communities.

References

Anyabwile, T. (2010) *The gospel for Muslims: An encouragement to share Christ with confidence.* Moody Publishers.

Bhatia, A. (2015). *Perspectives, attitudes and practices of American evangelicals towards Muslims in the U.S. Ph.D.* Dissertation. Trinity Evangelical Divinity School.

Boren, M. S. (2010). *Missional small groups: Becoming a community that makes a difference in the world.* Baker Books.

Breen, M. (2013). *Leading missional communities: Rediscovering the power of living on mission together,* Kindle Edition. 3 Dimension Ministries.

Foundation for Ethnic Understanding. (March 2019) Evangelical Christian and Muslim relations the U.S. https://ffeu.org/2019-study-on-evangelical-muslim-relations/

Green, L. C. (October 2015). Pastors grow more polarized on Islam. LifeWay Research. https://lifewayresearch.com/2015/10/22/pastors-grow-more-polarized-on-islam/

Gustafson, D. M. (2019). *Gospel witness: Evangelism in word and deed.* Eerdmans.

Jipp, J. W. (2017). *Saved by faith and hospitality.* Eerdmans.

Kronk, R., Daniels, G., Chapman, M., and Watson, J. (2017). Fruitful practices in ministry to the North American Muslim diaspora: A mixed-methods study," *Fruitful Practice Research.* https://nextmove.net/uploads/FP-Diaspora-report_FINAL.pdf

Masri, F. (2008) *Bridges: Christians connecting with Muslims.* Crescent Project.

McNeal, R. (2011). *Missional communities: The rise of the post-congregational church,* Kindle Edition, Jossey-Bass.

Mogahed, D., and Mahmood, A. (May 2019). American Muslim Poll 2019: Predicting and preventing Islamophobia. Institute for Social Policy and Understanding. https://www.ispu.org/american-muslim-poll-2019-full-report/

Mohamed, B. (2018). New estimates continue to show U.S. Muslim population continues to Grow. *Pew Forum.* https://www.pewresearch.org/fact- tank/2018/01/03/new-estimates-show-u-s-muslim-population-continues-to-grow/

Newbigin, L. (1989). *The gospel in a pluralist society*. Eerdmans.

Newbigin, L. (1995). *The open secret: An introduction to the theology of mission*. Eerdmans.

Netland, H. (2001) *Encountering religious pluralism: The challenge to Christian faith and mission*. InterVarsity Press.

Oksnevad, R. & Urton, M. (2014). *Journey to Jesus: Building Christ-centered friendships with Muslims*. Tyndale House Publishers.

Pew Forum (2017). Demographic portrait of Muslim Americans. http://www.pewforum.org/2017/07/26/demographic-portrait-of-muslim-americans/

Shellnut, K. (July 2017). Most while evangelicals don't think muslims belong in America. *Christianity Today.* http://www.christianitytoday.com/news/2017/july/pew-how-white-evangelicals-view-us-muslims-islam.html

Smith, J. (2013). Missional communities and community formation: What does the New Testament have to say? *Missio Apostolica, 21*(2), pp. 190-202.

Stetzer, E. (2018). Islam, North America, and the new multi-faith reality: How now shall we Live? In *Islam and North America: Loving our Muslim neighbors* (M. Fries and K. Whitfield, eds.), pp. 3-17. B&H Academic.

Urton, M. (2021). How evangelical churches in the Chicago Metro Area are engaging Muslim communities. Doctor of Ministry Project, Trinity Evangelical Divinity School.

About the Author

Rev. Mike Urton. D.Min., is the Director of Immigrant Mission for the EFCA. He has served among the Muslim and Muslim Background Believer population of Chicago for 20 years.

GREAT COMMISSION
RESEARCH JOURNAL
2022, Vol. 14(1) 51-68

The Continuity Mindset for Christian Mission

Jack Davison
South Asia

Abstract

Missionaries from the Global North regularly serve as trainers for Christians in the Global South. From personal experience, missionaries are regularly seen as being qualified to do this work simply because of their position. Rather than missionaries assuming they are competent purely on the basis of their titles, I believe they should instead practice the Continuity Mindset for Christian Mission, a mindset that emphasizes the continuity of one's identity and ministry in one's home culture with one's identity and ministry in the host culture. This practice includes elements of vulnerable mission, nonresidential mission, tentmaking, cultural intelligence, and authentic leadership. I propose that the intentional practice of the continuity mindset can help missionaries from the Global North appropriately fulfill training responsibilities or ambitions they may have in the Global South. This article introduces the continuity mindset and how its theoretical foundations can aid missionaries from the Global North in laying down their power in order to better serve those to whom they are sent in the Global South.

As my wife and I prepared to move overseas a decade ago, we noticed a shift had happened within our missions organization from emphasizing direct pioneer church planting among unreached people groups to instead searching for same-culture or near-culture partners to train to reach those groups.

Steffen (2011) and Schattner (2013) both confirm that this is happening in the broader missionary community as well, and several popular missions strategies involve the missionary spending significant time training local believers in evangelism, discipleship, and church planting (e.g., Addison, 2015; Smith & Kai, 2011; Watson & Watson, 2014). On a short-term mission trip prior to being sent long-term, I had already inadvertently leveraged my being a White American—all of 23 years old at the time with two whole weeks in the region—to train South Asians on the concept of Training for Trainers developed by Smith and Kai (2011). At the time, I thought I had simply been walking in the favor of the Lord to be given such an opportunity, but after moving back to the same city a year later and working in the region ever since, my understanding of that experience has drastically changed.

The common practice of missionaries from the Global North training Christians in the Global South is not necessarily bad, but one must ask why missionaries are often assumed to be capable of training believers in an entirely different part of the world. While it may be easy for Christians from the Global North to become self-proclaimed experts in church planting and ignore what people in the Global South have to teach them (Rynkiewich, 2016), it is hopefully obvious that missionaries from the Global North should not be considered as inherently qualified to train Christians in the Global South in evangelism, discipleship, and church planting. Followers of Jesus in the Global South have a rich Christian history that is often overlooked and ignored (Cooper, 2016; Jenkins, 2008), are the majority of believers in the world today (Zurlo et al., 2020), increasingly send out their own missionaries (Zurlo et al., 2021), and have much to offer to the Global North. In light of these facts, some may ask why anyone from the Global North should serve in any kind of capacity as a trainer in the Global South. This is a fair question, and a question with which I have wrestled. Since unreached people groups are mostly in the Global South (Zurlo et al., 2021), it still arguably makes sense that missionaries, from both regions, should focus on going there—even though this does not seem to be the case since missionaries are usually sent to countries with the greatest number of Christians (Zurlo et al., 2020, 2021). Nevertheless, since I believe God is still calling and sending people to share his message, I assume that this may involve missionaries from the Global North ending up as trainers in the Global South. However, I would not be surprised or discouraged if this number dwindles as more missionaries are sent from the Global South itself.

Being from the Global North, I propose that while missionaries from the Global North should never assume they are inherently capable of training believers in the Global South, neither must they forever avoid the practice. One way they might develop helpful—and I believe necessary—attitudes for such work is by practicing what I call the Continuity Mindset for Christian Mission, a mindset that emphasizes the continuity of one's identity and ministry in one's home culture with one's identity and ministry in the host culture. In this article, I hope to point out some flaws in the common missionary tactic of "defaulting to being trainers and imparters of Western knowledge, approaches, technologies, and systems" (Tizon, 2018, p. 51). I will describe the continuity mindset and its development and explain how the practices of the continuity mindset can help correct problematic paradigms.

Missionaries as Trainers

To begin, I want to clarify that the continuity mindset is proposed specifically for missionaries whose primary job description is to serve as a trainer for other believers. Missionaries who feel called and gifted to directly pioneer new ministry efforts in unreached locales, practice Business as Mission, or engage in development efforts may not find the continuity mindset especially relevant. With this in mind, it is important to look further at missionaries serving as trainers, including common practices and potential problems.

The Standard Operating Procedure

While preparing to serve in South Asia, my wife and I were taught that the most effective use of our time would be to train local believers how to reach the lost around them. As Smith and Kai (2011) say, "mobilizing and training existing Christians is a high value in CPMs [Church Planting Movements] all over the world" (The Scribe in the Kingdom section, para. 5). This is especially true for believers who are either from the targeted unreached people group or a similar group. Watson and Watson (2014) note several times the importance of training others in the various skills and activities necessary for disciple making. Addison (2015) encourages people hoping to see people movements to train as many people as possible since only a small percentage of the trained apply what they have learned outside of their current social network; by increasing the number of trainees—he implies that missionaries should think in terms of training thousands—then the number of disciple-makers will be sufficient to see an unreached people group reached.

Smith and Parks (2015) write that missionaries interested in seeing movements of people coming to faith should switch "from being church planters to being catalysts that empower reproducing churches to be started" (p. 37). Admittedly, several of the concepts discussed thus far are not without their critics. The concept of unreached people groups is somewhat controversial (e.g., Hendrickson, 2018; Lee & Park, 2018). Similarly, church planting or disciple-making movements, which are at the heart of Training for Trainers and other approaches to training done by missionaries from the Global North, are panned by many (e.g., Massey, 2012; Wu, 2014a, 2014b). In this article, it will be assumed that movements can be understood and used in biblical ways, though I will refrain from promoting any one particular methodology and concede that there are issues with some movement proponents' hermeneutics and statistics.

From my own experience, it seems fairly easy for missionaries from the Global North to find training opportunities in the Global South. Rynkiewich (2016) comments on how Christians from the Global North are quick "to try to partner, raise money, and provide training" (p. 314) when they hear of Christians in the Global South trying to accomplish a God-sized vision in their home nation. In many contexts, foreign missionaries are welcomed with open arms by local churches and given prominent roles and designations simply for showing up (Godwin & Mutter, 2013). Hibbert and Hibbert (2019) note "the tendency to impose a culturally alien pattern of leadership" (p. 242) by missionaries coming into new cultural settings. The Hibberts (2019) also note that foreign missionaries are able to make this kind of imposition because they are probably entering these settings with a significant amount of power. Baer (2020) argues that at least some Christians in the Global South feel that they are but pawns in missionaries' grand strategies, a means to bring about the foreigners' glorious end visions (p. 147)

Patron-Client Settings

The inherent power with which missionaries from the Global North arrive in the Global South is related to patronage. Georges (2019) asserts that the majority of the Global North are ignorant of how patron-client relationships function (p. 2) and defines patronage as

> a reciprocal relationship between a patron and a client. Patrons are the superior party with resources and power to help other people. ... Their generosity protects and provides for the people under their care.
>
> Clients, on the other hand, are social inferiors who attach themselves to a patron in order to secure protection and resources. ... But the client is not as wealthy as the patron, so instead of repaying financially, they repay by honoring the patron. A client offers obedience, gratitude, allegiance, and solidarity to the patron. (p. 9)

Unless the missionary is very intentional, simply being in an area can inadvertently put them in the role of patron for the local Christians, the clients, with whom they are working in their host nation (Dyer, 2017; Harries, 2019; Williams, 2019). In other words, they are now in a position of higher status in the relationships they have with local believers, perhaps without even realizing it. Needless to say, patronage is something that missionaries from the Global North must properly understand and consider if they are preparing to serve in areas where patronage is "the social 'operating system' that shapes relationships" (Georges, 2019, p. 2).

Colonialism and Neo-Colonialism

One may ask why missionaries from the Global North are expected to serve as patrons when they arrive in the Global South (Georges, 2019). The histories of the Christian missions enterprise and colonialism are entwined (Rynkiewich, 2011), though the exact nature of the relationship is debated. Woodberry (2009) argues that the presence of missionaries was generally beneficial to the indigenous peoples in the colonies—citing their influence in the spread of positive educational, scientific, medicinal, and social innovations—though he concedes negative anecdotes are easy to find. Tizon (2018) acknowledges the positive impact missionaries had in the time of colonialism, but also laments their role in enabling and propagating slavery (pp. 43-45). The echoes of colonialism are still resounding today.

Missionaries from the Global North often rely on funds from back home, which complicates their relationships with locals in a variety of ways (Alawode, 2020; Fox, 2006; Harries, 2021). This is particularly messy in the context of neocolonialism, the "apparent political independence but economic control from the outside" (Rynkiewich, 2011, p. 118), a reality that pervades much of the Global South. Kim (2010) writes that "world Christianity is deeply enmeshed within the current neocolonial systems and operations of power. A deeper question, then, is to what extent Christian missions...participate in reinforcing neocolonial realities or...resisting them" (p. 11). Missionaries from the Global North must recognize that colonialism, neocolonialism, and related historical and contemporary phenomena affect their relationships in much of the world.

What to Do?

If missionaries from the Global North can accept that they most likely arrive on the field with more power than the typical local Christian, then they should ponder what to do in light of this fact. I visited a missionary family in East Asia after they had been on the field for a relatively short time. They seemed discouraged and eventually shared that they had basically been advised by other missionaries from the Global North to leverage their White skin and English language skills to step into roles of influence in the community. Some could argue that leveraging the position of power for the greater good is appropriate. Certainly, patronage can be utilized, if understood appropriately, to be a blessing to others (Georges, 2019; Georges & Baker, 2016), so does it not follow that missionaries from the Global North should simply utilize their power to fulfill the calling God has placed on their lives?

One might argue that Paul used his Roman citizenship in a utilitarian fashion at times (e.g., Acts 16:37-39, 22:25-29), though I believe this is not quite analogous to the present discussion. Others might argue from Paul's declaration at the end of 1 Corinthians 9:22, "so that by all possible means I might save some" (NIV), that leveraging power to train and mobilize local believers in reaching unreached people groups is appropriate, though to do this would seemingly ignore the entire context of the whole passage in which Paul is discussing his having made himself "a slave to everyone, to win as many as possible" (1 Cor. 9:19, NIV).

On the whole, it seems difficult to argue against missionaries from the Global North laying down their power in order to better serve their new neighbors in the Global South. Since Jesus, "who, being in very nature God, did not consider equality with God something to be used to his own advantage" (Phil. 2:6, NIV), it seems like the burden of proof rests on those arguing in favor of missionaries holding onto power.

If missionaries from the Global North can accept that they have the responsibility to lay down their power, as Jesus himself did in his mission to humanity, then how might one go about doing that?

The Continuity Mindset for Christian Mission

I believe that practicing the continuity mindset will help missionaries develop the necessary attitudes to be trainers in the Global South. The main way it does so is by effectively enabling privileged missionaries from the Global North to surrender their power.

The continuity mindset's name stems from what I perceive to be a general lack of continuity between missionaries' lives at home and their lives abroad. For instance, upon moving to South Asia, I went from being an insider in my own community—speaking the same language as most of the people around me, having established relationships, and having a somewhat clear sense of identity—to being an outsider who did not speak the language, had no local friendships or history, and had no clue who I was anymore. I sometimes felt shunned as a foreigner while at other times celebrated; in either case, it felt difficult to develop relationships with people, even if I was onstage training an eager audience. I realized that by having two very disconnected and mutually irrelevant lives, I arrived with very little credibility other than my credentials of being a White American male. I eventually began to try integrating those two radically different parts of my life, using my experiences in one setting to assist what I was doing in the other, and thus establishing continuity between the two.

Part of this journey has been wrestling with the clear power imbalance that exists between myself and the South Asian people with whom I have interacted over the past decade. As a white male, it would be ignorant of me to claim that I experience no power imbalances in America, but I believe it happens less frequently in America than in South Asia. In both locations, Jesus' example calls me to lay down whatever power I have for the sake of others, though in South Asia it requires more effort since I am operating in radically different cultures from my home culture.

I have drawn from a variety of resources to tweak the missionary-as-trainer paradigm I inherited, including elements from vulnerable mission, nonresidential mission, tentmaking, cultural intelligence, and authentic leadership. By God's grace, as I began to pull from these different resources over the past few years, my closest South Asian friend and confidante noticed a significant positive difference between who I was when we met and who I have started to become.

I believe that if missionaries practice the continuity mindset by utilizing these different elements, then they can develop into the kind of people who are actually equipped to train believers in a variety of contexts without inadvertently abusing the dynamics involved in patron-client contexts or exacerbating lingering issues created and propagated by colonialism and its offspring. The following is a description of the fundamental elements of the continuity mindset.

Vulnerable Mission

According to Dyer (2017), the concept of vulnerable mission concerns missionaries from the Global North who "deliberately choose *not* to assert control, or take authority and power" (p. 39) over the local community by instead using the local language and avoiding the use of outside resources. Williams (2019) clarifies that "resources are not limited to money but include soft resources such as thinking styles" (The Alliance for Vulnerable Mission section). Looking to "the ultimate biblical example of vulnerability ... that of Christ in his incarnation" (Dyer, 2017, p. 42), proponents of vulnerable mission contend that vulnerability is the proper attitude for Christian missionaries.

Vulnerable mission is similar to other lines of missiological thought. Godwin and Mutter (2013) refer to what they call "incarnational practice" (p. 39) as their prescription for missionaries, inspired by Jesus' commission of his disciples in John 20:21, "As the Father has sent me, I am sending you" (NIV, 2011). Broadly defined, this looks like embracing "sacrifice ... [by] setting aside one's own ambitions, agenda, timing, protocol, and expectations in the service of national partners" (Godwin & Mutter, 2013, p. 41). Baer (2020) describes the ideal missionary as a "fellow traveller" (p. 142) and believes learning the local language is "the most important thing" (p. 142) in becoming one. Learning the local language puts the missionary in a position of vulnerability where they desperately need the help of their hosts (Baer, 2020).

I remember upon arrival in South Asia being encouraged by welcoming missionaries to not bother learning the local language since English was widely spoken and it would permit that my wife and I hit the ground running. Thankfully, we had other friends and colleagues saying the opposite, so we spent three years in full-time language study. Not only did we learn the local language, but we also learned that the use of English was not quite as effective as some of the other missionaries had claimed; we also learned a lot about the culture since some things could not easily be translated or understood clearly in English. Beyond the language and cultural acquisition, we also learned a type of humility that I do not believe we could have otherwise. As Baer (2020) implies, learning a language can be humiliating, which goes a long way in helping missionaries learn that they are not the star of the show.

Nonresidential Mission

The idea of the nonresidential missionary emerged in the late 1980s, at least within the Southern Baptist denomination (Carlton, 2006; Garrison, 1990). Garrison (1990) defines a nonresidential missionary as "a full-time, professional career foreign missionary who is matched up with a single unevangelized population segment...for purposes of concentrating on priorities of initial evangelization and eliminating gaps and inadvertent duplications with other agencies" (p. 13) while residing, as the name suggests, "outside the targeted assignment because legal residence for a missionary is either prohibited or highly restricted" (p. 13). Their nonresidential status and high intentionality in partnering with other Christians to reach a particular unreached people group are considered distinctives (Garrison, 1990, p. 14). A nonresidential missionary has "a firm commitment to strategic planning" (Carlton, 2006, p. 60) in terms of networking with other believers in reaching an unreached people group. Presently, within the Southern Baptist denomination, the term nonresidential missionary has been replaced with *strategy coordinator* (Carlton, 2006).

Obviously, the world has changed since Garrison's (1990) initial proposal, and while security concerns are still relevant today, there are other reasons to implement this practice. The nonresidential missionary or strategy coordinator role for Southern Baptists would eventually include a focus on catalyzing movements by working with local Christians, as well as the understanding that the foreigner needed "an exit strategy" (Carlton, 2006, p. 211). This thinking mirrors Watson and Watson's (2014) belief that "great delegators know how to take their hands off in order to create a leadership vacuum that potential leaders will fill if given the chance" (p. 185). The fact that Jesus and Paul were consistently itinerant (Wolff, 2004) also lends credence to the need for creating leadership vacuums.

It seems clear that Jesus' earthly ministry was less than three years in duration (Votaw, 1905), and from what is clearly mentioned in Acts, Paul's longest duration in any place after being sent out from Antioch seems to have been three years in Ephesus (Acts 20:31). I submit that at least one of the reasons Jesus and Paul did not stay longer in any particular place is that they were essentially throwing people into the water and trusting the Holy Spirit to help them swim. If anyone could successfully allow people to depend on them, I think it would be Jesus, and yet Jesus clearly told his disciples, "but very truly I tell you, it is for your good that I am going away. Unless I go away, the Advocate will not come to you; but if I go, I will send him to you" (John 16:7,

NIV). Allen (1962) writes that Paul "believed in the Holy Ghost, not merely vaguely as a spiritual Power, but as a Person indwelling his converts. He believed therefore in his converts. ... he believed in the Holy Ghost in them" (p. 149). Paul recognized a missionary's task was one of planting and watering, "but only God ... makes things grow" (1 Cor 3:7), and he actively fought against people becoming overly attached to him (e.g., 1 Cor 1:10-17; 3:1-23).

Beyond the security and logistical benefits of working as a nonresidential missionary, I believe the most overwhelming benefit is how it can be used to prevent the missionary from becoming the center of the story, a place that should be left for God alone. This is not to say that extended residence in a foreign country can be omitted fully; it may be quite necessary early in a missionary's career to learn language and culture, two critical components of practicing vulnerable mission. Jesus spent around 30 years on earth before beginning his public ministry (Luke 3:23), and there is at least a decade of near-silence on Paul's activities in Tarsus and Antioch between his conversion in Acts 9 and his being sent out in Acts 11 (Gal 2:1).

Nonresidential mission does not imply that ongoing communication ceases between the nonresidential missionary and their local contacts. Jesus promised the Holy Spirit would continue to communicate on his behalf to his disciples (John 16:12-14). Several of the books in the New Testament are examples of Paul's ongoing communication with his friends while he was not physically present, and he was intentional to follow up with these communities in person (e.g., Acts 15:36). Regular communication via the Internet and in-person visits will be normal, especially since authentic relationships have ideally formed between missionaries and their local co-laborers.

In my own experience, my family and I began to consider adopting a nonresidential missionary strategy in light of security concerns in our former location; after spending time talking with nonresidential missionaries and studying the ministries of Jesus and Paul, I began to realize the additional potential benefits of becoming nonresidential. We had the privilege of living in South Asia for a significant length of time before relocating to a nearby country due to security issues. We sensed that such a move would allow for greater fruitfulness in South Asia. Within six months of our departure, things we had helped build fell apart; while at first discouraging, we soon realized that this was revealing how much of the ministry had depended on our physical presence. While we had been intentional to practice vulnerable mission while living in South Asia, we found there was no substitute for simply getting out of the way. Although the last few years have been intermittently painful as we interact with our friends from afar—along with regular in-person visits—we are thankful that God has become more central in the story of our friends' lives, and we are confident and full of faith that the Holy Spirit will continue to grow what we have planted and watered.

Tentmaking

I refer to tentmaking as something separate from Business as Mission, though the terms are related and at times conflated (Johnson & Rundle, 2006). Johnson and Rundle (2006) specifically define a tentmaker "as a mission-minded Christian who supports himself or herself in a cross-cultural mission context through a vocation such as teaching English, medical work, or working for a locally-owned or international company" (pp. 23-24). My experience concurs with Johnson and Rundle's claim that many long-term missionaries view tentmaking "as a necessary evil" (p. 24), usually only undertaken as means of obtaining a visa for residing in a foreign country. In the missionary community, I frequently hear this referred to as a platform, a bare minimum job that provides a visa; the less time and energy involved, the better. Initially, I certainly fell into this category, and I now shake my head in embarrassment when I remember explaining our platform to South Asians because it made no sense to them why my family would move across the world to work for what was more or less a shell company.

While there are practical benefits to having a non-ministry job in a foreign country for missionaries, there are also other benefits to tentmaking that should be considered even in countries where it is not logistically required (Malone, 2014). Russell (2006) lists three reasons that Paul made tents: to identify with his target people, to demonstrate that he was credible and "cared more about his message than his money" (p. 169), and to model a life of a regular disciple who is not a professional Christian. On the first point, it is important to remember that identification is a two-way street—Paul was able to better understand his audience, but they could also more readily identify with him. Paul's work as a tentmaker also freed him from having to become a client to a human patron (Georges, 2019; Lohr, 2007), thus avoiding obligations that could potentially derail his ministry goals.

With all of the above in mind, I understand a tentmaker as a missionary who has a legitimate, income-providing job in their country of residence, without that job being their primary focus; unlike my former platform job in South Asia, this job is appropriate for the particular missionary given their education and work experience. Due to the focus of these missionaries on reaching unreached people groups, it is unlikely that this job can be full-time, meaning that at least part of the missionary's salary may continue to come from the financial support of believers back home. But I believe such a job can still be useful, beyond providing visas and a partial salary.

For example, after leaving our home in South Asia, I began to work in a field in our current country of residence that aligned with my prior job experience in the United States. It has been a breath of fresh air to not dread being asked about my work. While I definitely benefit from the part-time salary and visa the job provides, I have appreciated the extra benefits mentioned by Russell (2006) even more. I now make sense to everyone I meet;

people are not confused why I would live in a foreign country since I have legitimate employment. The job also places me within a community that includes families who speak the same language as the one I had previously learned and has enabled my family to spend time in South Asian neighborhoods without suspicion.

Having a non-ministry job has also paid off in terms of training Christians since they see that I am bivocational. Before, I would encourage local believers whom I had trained to be bivocational since raising financial support for their ministries was not viable in their location. Essentially, I was telling people, who knew I did little work on my platform, to do as I said, not as I did. When I now encourage pastors to look for part-time work, I actually know what working bi-vocationally means and have paid the associated time and energy costs myself.

Finally, tentmaking may also help missionaries in their practice of vulnerable mission. As one missionary from the Global North shared with me, working in a formal position in her host country under local leadership was a transformative experience as it enabled her to avoid coming into her location in a position of power. In my own experience over the past few years, working in a formal role under someone from the Global South has taught me how to serve someone else's vision rather than only knowing how to have other people serve mine.

Cultural Intelligence

Cultural intelligence is "an individual's capability to function and manage effectively in culturally diverse settings" (Ang & Van Dyne, 2008, p. 3). While the legitimacy of cultural intelligence as a definable, measurable, and universal construct is not without question (Berry & Ward, 2006; Blasco et al., 2012), a high level of cultural intelligence has been shown to have a positive impact on intercultural effectiveness (Deng & Gibson, 2008; Ersoy, 2014; Rockstuhl et al., 2011), and the research seems to typically reflect positive sentiments towards the construct (Fang et al., 2018). One key premise of cultural intelligence is that it is "malleable" (Van Dyne et al., 2012, p. 303) and can be intentionally developed over time.

Learning about different cultural value dimensions—like individualism versus collectivism, high versus low power distance, and long-term versus short-term orientation—such as those described by Hofstede et al. (2010) or the Global Leadership and Organizational Behavior Effectiveness program (House et al., 2004) can increase cultural intelligence and may be useful in combatting ethnocentrism (Northouse, 2019). Critiques of the use of cultural value dimensions often include the dangers of stereotyping and unfairly or incorrectly predicting someone else's behavior based on various cultural value scales (Beugelsdijk et al., 2017; Brewer & Venaik, 2012; Venaik & Brewer, 2013). While I agree that stereotyping is dangerous and that cultural value dimensions should not be used to indiscriminately box people in, I also think Richards and O'Brien's (2012) suggestion cannot be ignored: "Generalizations are always wrong and usually helpful" (p. 19).

As I have intentionally developed my own cultural intelligence, I have appreciated the benefits of being able to anticipate rather than predict the concerns and behaviors of others from different cultural backgrounds. I use the verb *anticipate* to convey a cautious use of cultural value dimensions that includes an awareness that every person is unique and will not fit all of their cultural norms. Rather than only having my own cultural background as a context for understanding my friends from the Global South, through developing cultural intelligence I have added awareness of other cultural backgrounds. For example, while the South Asian profile of the Global Leadership and Organizational Behavior Effectiveness study (House et al., 2004) may be inaccurate in some respects, knowing that my South Asian friends are likely to be more collectivist than my American individualist self is obviously critical in order for me to better understand them.

Being culturally intelligent also enables people to know when to accept the roadmap of a foreign culture and when to reject it (Livermore, 2015). Going back to the topic of patronage mentioned above, Georges (2019) notes that Paul purposefully avoided taking on clients in Corinth; "the source of the Corinthians' honor was not their relationship with Paul (as either his patron or his client) but their connection with God" (p. 65). In other settings, however, Paul did engage in a different form of patronage where God was understood as the ultimate patron, and Paul and his companions were on equal footing as clients; "healthy patron-client relationships were possible because Paul discipled early Christians into a transformed view of patronage, as seen in 2 Corinthians 8-9 and Philippians 4" (Georges, 2019, p. 67). Paul's knowledge of the culture in which he ministered allowed him to appropriately interact with cultural norms to most effectively honor God and serve those around him.

Personally, developing cultural intelligence has helped my family handle cultural stress and form strong friendships in the Global South. Rather than forcing people into stereotypes in my mind, I have found that cultural intelligence has enabled me to understand how and when people either do or do not fit their cultural norms, as well as explain my own points of view and opinions on important subjects without being misunderstood because of cultural differences.

Authentic Leadership

This last point regarding cultural intelligence, communicating effectively across cultures, is worthy of further discussion. In addition to skepticism regarding cultural intelligence as a construct, arguments have been made that it is a tool that allows people to "manipulate cultural values and mores in order to serve the agendas" (M. J. Dutta & Dutta, 2013, p. 252) of the Global North rather than actually serving people in the Global South. Basically, some could interpret my increased effectiveness in intercultural communication as actually increased cleverness at getting my way in relationships with people from the Global South. I must admit that I find this line of reasoning fairly compelling, though I do believe there are safeguards to this abuse of cultural intelligence. Vulnerable mission is obviously helpful in making sure cultural intelligence is used to lovingly serve, rather than selfishly control, others, but practicing authentic leadership may provide even more concrete guiderails to ensure missionaries do not get off track.

Vogelgesang and colleagues (2009) include a description of the four components of authentic leadership when they propose that

> authentic leaders—who possess a deep understanding of their actions and feelings (self-awareness), who have the ability to weigh information from both internal and external sources when making decisions about behavior (balanced processing), who have created an open dialogue with their followers (relational transparency), and whose decisions and actions stem from the morals developed within the culture of one's home country (moral perspective)—will be able to exhibit morally grounded cultural adaptation. (p. 104).

In other words, practicing authentic leadership enables culturally intelligent individuals to maintain alignment with their values or moral perspective. At the same time, cultural intelligence should help an "authentic leader...more fully comprehend the differences between the host culture values and his or her own deeply held beliefs" (Vogelgesang et al., 2009, p. 104). A culturally intelligent authentic leader should be able to maintain their values—such as loving God and avoiding sin—and adjust their culturally conditioned understandings of those values as appropriate, such as worship style preferences or how they demonstrate love for neighbors. Combining cultural intelligence and authentic leadership can help someone working in intercultural settings understand "what behaviour can be adapted without jeopardizing authenticity and what behaviour must align with...[their] own cultural values, thereby remaining authentic" (Green, 2017, p. 265).

A culturally unintelligent authentic leader may not discern whether something is in conflict with their inner values or is simply a new and different experience, such as a missionary from an individualist culture with a strong value for truth-telling not being able to understand why someone in a collectivist culture might use a more indirect communication style (Hofstede et al., 2010). Truth can be shared both directly and indirectly, but not being aware of the cultural values surrounding indirect communication may lead the culturally unintelligent authentic leader to assume an indirect person is simply lying. Not only may they misunderstand the people around them, but they will almost certainly be misunderstood if they insist on speaking directly in that context.

On the other hand, a culturally intelligent missionary who has not intentionally developed a strong value system may inadvertently adapt to inappropriate behaviors and expectations in a foreign culture, as Vogelgesang et al. (2009) warn. This could look like assimilating into a sinful aspect of the host culture or the aforementioned misuse of cultural values to deceptively get others to do what they want (Dutta & Dutta, 2017; Dutta & Dutta, 2013).

Besides the moral perspective and relational transparency components of authentic leadership, self-awareness and balanced processing—"an individual's ability to analyze information objectively and explore other people's opinions before making a decision" (Northouse, 2019, p. 204)—fit easily into the cultural intelligence framework under one of its subdimensions, metacognitive cultural intelligence, which focuses on growing in self- and other-awareness (Livermore, 2015, pp. 29, 144-147). For missionaries from the Global North living in the Global South, practicing cultural intelligence or authentic leadership separately may be unadvisable; however, using the two concepts together seems like it may enable a more complete and effective practice of both.

Conclusion

Missionaries from the Global North training Christians in the Global South has proven to be fruitful in terms of catalyzing movements (Schattner, 2013), so it seems foolish to abandon the approach altogether. However, past fruitfulness should not blind missionaries' eyes to the real problems associated with the power that those from the Global North typically possess. Missionaries can glean from vulnerable mission, nonresidential mission, tentmaking, cultural intelligence, and authentic leadership to begin practicing the continuity mindset, which I believe is an effective way to create a link between a missionary's life at home and life abroad.

References

Addison, S. (2015). *Pioneering movements: Leadership that multiplies disciples and churches*. IVP Books. https://amz.run/4cwh

Alawode, A. O. (2020). The importance and challenges of money in Christian missions. *HTS Teologiese Studies/Theological Studies*, *76*(1), 1–5. https://doi.org/10.4102/hts.v76i1.5984

Allen, R. (1962). *Missionary methods: St. Paul's or ours?* (6th ed.). Wm. B. Eerdmans Publishing Co.

Ang, S., & Van Dyne, L. (2008). Conceptualization of cultural intelligence: Definition, distinctiveness, and nomological network. In S. Ang & L. Van Dyne (Eds.), *Handbook of cultural intelligence: Theory, measurement, and applications* (pp. 3–13). M.E. Sharpe, Inc. https://doi.org/10.4324/9781315703855

Baer, H. C. (2020). On Becoming a Fellow Traveller in Mission. *Evangelical Review of Theology, 44*(2), 141–148.

Berry, J. W., & Ward, C. (2006). Commentary on "redefining interactions across cultures and organizations." *Group and Organization Management, 31*(1), 64–77. https://doi.org/10.1177/1059601105275264

Beugelsdijk, S., Kostova, T., & Roth, K. (2017). An overview of Hofstede-inspired country-level culture research in international business since 2006. *Journal of International Business Studies, 48*(1), 30–47. https://doi.org/10.1057/s41267-016-0038-8

Blasco, M., Feldt, L. E., & Jakobsen, M. (2012). If only cultural chameleons could fly too: A critical discussion of the concept of cultural intelligence. *International Journal of Cross Cultural Management, 12*(2), 229–245. https://doi.org/10.1177/1470595812439872

Brewer, P., & Venaik, S. (2012). On the misuse of national culture dimensions. *International Marketing Review, 29*(6), 673–683. https://doi.org/10.1108/02651331211277991

Carlton, R. B. (2006). *An analysis of the impact of the non-residential/strategy coordinator's role in Southern Baptist missiology* (Publication No. 0818833) [Doctoral dissertation, University of South Africa]. ProQuest Dissertations and Theses Global.

Cooper, D. (2016). *Introduction to world Christian history*. InterVarsity Press.

Deng, L., & Gibson, P. (2008). A qualitative evaluation on the role of cultural intelligence in cross-cultural leadership effectiveness. *International Journal of Leadership Studies, 3*(2), 181–197.

Dutta, D., & Dutta, M. J. (2017). Cultural intelligence, postcolonial critique. In Y. Y. Kim & K. L. McKay-Semmler (Eds.), *The international encyclopedia of intercultural communication* (pp. 1–7). John Wiley & Sons, Inc. https://doi.org/10.1002/9781118783665.ieicc0212

Dutta, M. J., & Dutta, D. (2013). Multinational going cultural: A postcolonial deconstruction of cultural intelligence. In *Journal of International and Intercultural Communication* (Vol. 6, Issue 3, pp. 241–258). https://doi.org/10.1080/17513057.2013.790989

Dyer, A. E. (2017). A discussion of vulnerability in mission for the twenty-first century from a biblical perspective. *Transformation, 34*(1), 38–49. https://doi.org/10.1177/0265378816631253

Ersoy, A. (2014). The role of cultural intelligence in cross-cultural leadership effectiveness: A qualitative study in the hospitality industry. *Journal of Yasar University, 9*(35), 6099–6108.

Fang, F., Schei, V., & Selart, M. (2018). Hype or hope? A new look at the research on cultural intelligence. *International Journal of Intercultural Relations, 66*, 148–171. https://doi.org/10.1016/j.ijintrel.2018.04.002

Fox, F. F. (2006). Foreign money for India: Antidependency and anticonversion perspectives. *International Bulletin of Missionary Research, 30*(3), 137–142. https://doi.org/10.1177/239693930603000305

Garrison, V. D. (1990). *The nonresidential missionary*. MARC.

Georges, J. (2019). *Ministering in patronage cultures: Biblical models and missional implications*. InterVarsity Press. https://amz.run/4Usy

Georges, J., & Baker, M. D. (2016). *Ministering in honor-shame cultures: Biblical foundations and practical essentials*. InterVarsity Press. https://amz.run/4ffY

Godwin, C., & Mutter, K. F. (2013). Hero, privilege, partnership, incarnational practice: Examining the narratives of missionary practice. *McMaster Journal of Theology and Ministry, 15*, 17–50.

Green, M. J. (2017). Adaptation versus authenticity: Achieving leader effectiveness in intercultural encounters with followers – towards an integrated model. *International Journal of Cross Cultural Management, 17*(2), 257–271. https://doi.org/10.1177/1470595817706986

Harries, J. (2019). Essential alternatives to contemporary missionary training: For the sake of vulnerability to the majority world (Africa). *Transformation, 36*(4), 266–279. https://doi.org/10.1177/0265378819844537

Harries, J. (2021). Re-strategising mission (and development) intervention into Africa to avoid corruption, the prosperity gospel and missionary ignorance. *Transcending Mission: The Eclipse of a Modern Tradition*, 1–14. https://doi.org/10.1177/0265378821994595

Hendrickson, C. S. (2018). Ending racial profiling in the church: Revisiting the homogenous unit principle. *Mission Studies, 35*(3), 342–365. https://doi.org/10.1163/15733831-12341589

Hibbert, R., & Hibbert, E. (2019). Defining culturally appropriate leadership. *Missiology: An International Review, 47*(3), 240–251. https://doi.org/10.1177/0091829619858595

Hofstede, G., Hofstede, G. J., & Minkov, M. (2010). *Cultures and organizations: Software of the mind* (3rd ed.). McGraw-Hill. https://amz.run/42ac

House, R. J., Hanges, P. J., Javidan, M., Dorfman, P. W., & Gupta, V. (Eds.). (2004). *Culture, leadership, and organizations: The GLOBE study of 62 societies*. SAGE Publications, Inc. https://amz.run/4O7G

Jenkins, P. (2008). *The lost history of Christianity: The thousand-year golden age of the church in the Middle East, Africa, and Asia--And how it died.* HarperCollins.

Johnson, N., & Rundle, S. (2006). Distinctives and challenges of business as mission. In T. Steffen & M. Barnett (Eds.), *Business as mission: From impoverished to empowered* (pp. 20–46). William Carey Library. https://amz.run/4fxe

Kim, N. (2010). A mission to the "graveyard of empires"? Neocolonialism and the contemporary evangelical missions of the global south. *Mission Studies, 27*(1), 3–23. https://doi.org/10.1163/157338310X497946

Lee, P. T., & Park, J. S.-H. (2018). Beyond people group thinking: A critical reevaluation of unreached people groups. *Missiology: An International Review, 46*(3), 212–225. https://doi.org/10.1177/0091829618774332

Livermore, D. (2015). *Leading with cultural intelligence: The real secret to success* (2nd ed.). American Management Association. https://amz.run/42af

Lohr, J. N. (2007). He Identified with the lowly and became a slave to all: Paul's tentmaking as a strategy for mission. *Currents in Theology and Mission, 34*(3), 179–187.

Malone, K. (2014). Broadening the tent: Expanding the strategic use of tentmaking in cross-cultural mission. *Missiology: An International Review, 42*(2), 195–206. https://doi.org/10.1177/0091829613507022

Massey, J. D. (2012). Wrinkling time in the missionary task: A theological review of church planting movements methodology. *Southwestern Journal of Theology, 55*(1), 100–137.

Northouse, P. G. (2019). *Leadership: Theory and practice* (8th ed.). SAGE Publications, Inc.

Richards, E. R., & O'Brien, B. J. (2012). *Misreading Scripture with Western eyes: Removing cultural blinders to better understand the Bible*. InterVarsity Press. https://amz.run/4RsW

Rockstuhl, T., Seiler, S., Ang, S., Van Dyne, L., & Annen, H. (2011). Beyond general intelligence (IQ) and emotional intelligence (EQ): The role of cultural intelligence (CQ) on cross-border leadership effectiveness in a globalized world. *Journal of Social Issues, 67*(4), 825–840. https://doi.org/10.1111/j.1540-4560.2011.01730.x

Russell, M. L. (2006). The biblical basis for the integration of business and missions. In T. Steffen & M. Barnett (Eds.), *Business as mission: From impoverished to empowered* (pp. 161–181). William Carey Library. https://amz.run/4fxe

Rynkiewich, M. A. (2011). *Soul, self, and society: A postmodern anthropology for mission in a postcolonial world*. Cascade Books.

Rynkiewich, M. A. (2016). "Do not remember the former things." *International Bulletin of Missionary Research, 40*(4), 308–317. https://doi.org/10.1177/2396939316656792

Schattner, F. W. (2013). *Sustainability within church planting movements in East Asia*. (Publication No. 3560649) [Doctoral dissertation, Biola University]. ProQuest Dissertations and Theses Global.

Smith, S., & Kai, Y. (2011). *T4T: A discipleship re-revolution*. WIGTake Resources. https://amz.run/4cwg

Smith, S., & Parks, S. (2015). T4T or DMM (DBS)? *Mission Frontiers, Jan/Feb*, 2–5. http://www.missionfrontiers.org/

Steffen, T. (2011). *The facilitator era: Beyond pioneer church multiplication*. Wipf & Stock. https://amz.run/4aZs

Tizon, A. (2018). *Whole and reconciled: Gospel, church, and mission in a fractured world*. Baker Academic.

Van Dyne, L., Ang, S., Ng, K. Y., Rockstuhl, T., Tan, M. L., & Koh, C. (2012). Sub-dimensions of the four factor model of cultural intelligence: Expanding the conceptualization and measurement of cultural intelligence. *Social and Personality Psychology Compass*, *6*(4), 295–313. https://doi.org/10.1111/j.1751-9004.2012.00429.x

Venaik, S., & Brewer, P. (2013). Critical issues in the Hofstede and GLOBE national culture models. *International Marketing Review*, *30*(5), 469–482. https://doi.org/10.1108/IMR-03-2013-0058

Vogelgesang, G., Clapp-Smith, R., & Palmer, N. (2009). The role of authentic leadership and cultural intelligence in cross-cultural contexts: An objectivist perspective. *International Journal of Leadership Studies*, *5*(2), 102–117.

Votaw, C. W. (1905). The chronology of Jesus' public ministry. *The Biblical World*, *26*(6), 425–430.

Watson, D. L., & Watson, P. D. (2014). *Contagious disciple making: Leading others on a journey of discovery*. Thomas Nelson. https://amz.run/4cwf

Williams, D. (2019). Toward a worldwide theology of vulnerable mission. *Missio Dei: A Journal of Missional Theology and Praxis*, *10*(2). http://missiodeijournal.com/issues/md-10-2/authors/md-10-2-williams

Wolff, C. (2004). Humility and self-denial in Jesus' life and message and in the apostolic existence of Paul. In A. J. M. Wedderburn (Ed.), *Paul and Jesus* (pp. 145–160). T&T Clark International.

Woodberry, R. D. (2009). The social impact of Christian missions. In *Perspectives on the world Christian movement: A reader* (4th ed., pp. 286–290). William Carey Library.

Wu, J. (2014a). The influence of culture on the evolution of mission methods: Using "church planting movements" as a case study. *Global Missiology*, *1*(12).

Wu, J. (2014b). There are no church planting movements in the Bible: Why biblical exegesis and missiological methods cannot be separated. *Global Missiology*, *1*(12).

Zurlo, G. A., Johnson, T. M., & Crossing, P. F. (2020). World Christianity and mission 2020: Ongoing shift to the Global South. *International Bulletin of Mission Research*, *44*(1), 8–19. https://doi.org/10.1177/2396939319880074

Zurlo, G. A., Johnson, T. M., & Crossing, P. F. (2021). World Christianity and mission 2021: Questions about the future. *International Bulletin of Mission Research*, *45*(1), 15–25. https://doi.org/10.1177/2396939320966220

About the Author

Jack T. Davison (pseudonym) has lived and worked in South and Southeast Asia for the last decade, focusing on helping local followers of Jesus make disciples who make disciples.

GREAT COMMISSION
RESEARCH JOURNAL
2022, Vol. 14(1) 69-85

The Sinner's Prayer: An Inappropriate Ritual for Thai Christian Culture and a Suggested Replacement

Kelly M. Hilderbrand
Bangkok Bible Seminary

Abstract

The practice of encouraging seekers to say the sinner's prayer has become commonplace in Thailand. However, the practice is relatively recent and has developed out of Western individualistic assumptions. It is not an explicitly biblical practice and has serious practical problems, producing decisions for Christ that often do not result in a long-term commitment to Christianity. The practice also runs counter to many Thai cultural norms and can be harmful to evangelism and discipleship in Thailand. This article suggests a different approach, the prayer challenge.

Introduction

Several years ago, I had a disturbing discussion with a young woman. She claimed her brother was a Christian. I asked if he went to church. He did not. I asked if he was walking with the Lord. He was not. His life choices demonstrated very clearly that he was not in a right relationship with Jesus or the Christian community. However, this woman insisted that her brother was a Christian because he had said the "sinner's prayer." In her mind, the very act of saying the prayer sealed his eternal fate. She is not alone in her conviction.

Evangelists in Thailand will often report, after conducting a revival meeting or preaching a sermon in a village or town, that many people have been "saved" or "made a decision for Jesus." Some of these claims run into the hundreds or thousands of people who have prayed a prayer of commitment to Jesus. I have been present for many of these events, in schools, in remote villages, and even in large cities. Usually, the event will last several days with a foreigner preaching the gospel through a translator. At the end of every sermon, at least in the evening service, the foreigner will call for people to raise their hands as a sign of commitment to follow Jesus. These people are then asked to pray with the preacher a prayer that is commonly referred to as the "sinner's prayer." Thai Christians have adopted this practice, encouraging seekers to pray the prayer to become a "Christian."

The purpose of this article is to explain why this practice is, at best, inappropriate for the Thai cultural context. Some scholars have suggested that this practice, in any cultural context, has biblical, theological, and practical issues that need to be addressed (Bennett, 2011; Chitwood 2001; Dahlfred, 2020; Hulse, 2006; Martin & Visser 2012; Murray, 1973). Scholars with experience in Thailand have also noted that the practice can be counterproductive to Thai evangelism and discipleship (Dahlfred, 2020; Martin & Visser 2012). Chitwood (2001), in his dissertation on the topic, has argued that the practice has produced many "converts," but very few disciples (p. 109). My concern for the ritual arose through my own experiences of its failings and flaws as a long-term missionary, pastor, and now seminary professor in Thailand.

At a large university in Bangkok, Thailand, a young Western woman from a well-known campus ministry was sharing the gospel on campus. On one typical hot and humid Bangkok day, this eager and sincere woman was sharing the gospel with a female Thai university student who had a rudimentary grasp of English. The young Thai woman listened patiently to the Western missionary as she explained the Four Spiritual Laws and the need to invite Jesus into her heart. At the end of the presentation, the devout Western missionary boldly invited the young Thai woman to pray the sinner's prayer with her and to become a Christian. With bowed head and while holding hands, the Thai woman repeated after the missionary the words of the prayer. After declaring the amen, the missionary explained to the young Thai woman that she was now a Christian. She should turn her back on her old ways, on the ways of Buddhism, find a Christian church, and grow in Christ.

Later that same day, this young Thai woman, who had prayed the sinner's prayer, found a Thai friend of hers who happened to be a Thai Christian and a member of my Bangkok church. The new "convert" expressed plainly how she now hated Christians and wanted nothing to do with Jesus. This woman felt used and abused by the Western missionary. She had been forced to pray to a god she did not know and change her religion. She renounced her prayer and this foreign religion.

Why did this happen? The Western missionary was, with a sincere heart and passion for the lost, trying to explain the gospel. In her mind, she did not force the young student to pray a prayer against her will. What went wrong? Cross-cultural ministry is a minefield and without a full understanding of the cultural context and language, many missionaries can step into very explosive situations without ever realizing what went wrong. I doubt that this Western missionary ever realized that by saying the sinner's prayer with this Thai woman, she had not won a convert but created an enemy.

In analyzing what went wrong, we must understand that Thai people are imbued from a young age with the concept of *krengjai*. This cultural affect is hard to explain to foreigners. However, in simplistic terms, a Thai person will always error on the side of politeness and submission in an interpersonal situation. Foreigners may see this as dishonest because a Thai person will not always tell you what they are thinking. Thai people see it as being polite and respectful.

The young Thai woman could not culturally refuse the invitation to pray with the female Westerner without being rude. The missionary was a religious worker. Therefore, the missionary had status. The young Thai woman prayed the prayer to be polite and to show deference to the foreign religious worker. However, she was enraged by the encounter.

In another example, missionary Karl Dahlfred (2020) wrote about his experience of church planting in a small town in Thailand. Over the course of two weeks, fifteen Thai Buddhists with no prior knowledge of the gospel came to the new church and prayed to receive Jesus. The Thai pastor was ecstatic. Small groups were formed to disciple these "new believers." But over the course of two months, all those "new believers" stopped attending the small groups and church. Had they lost their salvation? Were they not saved to begin with? The Thai pastor was now devastated. What had gone wrong?

During revival meetings in remote villages and towns, Thai people will automatically raise their hands when a call for a decision is made. The hands are raised so the foreigner will not lose face or feel embarrassed. They will pray with the evangelist out of respect for his learning and to honor the sacrifice made to travel to their village. Hands will rise all over the assembled crowd. The evangelist will be elated that so many people have now become Christian.

Most villagers have little to no concept of who Jesus is. In their worldview, Jesus is a powerful god, but a god of the foreigners, not the Thai. They may believe that Jesus answers prayers and even heals disease, but most attendees raising their hands are not instantly changing their religious allegiance. I am not saying that God is not working among those listening to the message nor am I limiting the power of God to change lives through the hearing of the gospel message. All I am saying is that the raising of hands or the saying of the sinner's prayer is not a good indication of true salvation or commitment to

Jesus. Jesus might be received as another god that the villagers consult if they have a problem, but no commitment has been made to Jesus as Savior and unique Lord. Those responding may not even understand those concepts.

One ministry in Thailand has claimed over 200,000 decisions for Christ since 2007. Although I support this ministry and believe that people are becoming Christian and churches are being started through their work, I believe their numbers are misleading. Thailand has approximately 505,000 evangelical Christians in the country as of April 2021 (eSTAR Foundation). If over 200,000 people chose to follow Christ through their ministry, then this one ministry is responsible for almost 40% of all Christians in the kingdom.

Before we fault this ministry, most ministries in Thailand report "decisions for Christ" in a similar fashion. Many churches supported by foreign mission organizations require churches to report the "number of salvations" each month or year. Raised hands are counted. People are encouraged to say the sinner's prayer. Numbers bring funding which is necessary for the ministry to continue.

In the best of circumstances, a skilled local Thai pastor will follow up with people after a sermon or evangelistic event to help seekers understand more. However, without follow-up and discipleship, most of these Thai "converts" simply do not have enough information to become a Christian by responding to a single sermon or presentation of the gospel. Follow-up and relationship development are needed.

This ritual is not just practiced by foreign missionaries. Thai pastors and Thai Christians have also adopted this practice. Seekers who show interest in learning more about Jesus are encouraged to pray a prayer of repentance and acceptance of Jesus. This prayer is called "*atithaan rap chua*" (อธิษฐานรับเชื่อ) in the Thai language, literally, a prayer to believe.

I cannot count the number of times I have heard someone say in a Thai church, "she said the prayer! She is a Christian now." The assumption is that saying the prayer is what brought salvation. The belief among many is that these ritual words bring someone from death to life. It is my conviction that this Western ritual should not be endorsed by the Thai church as it can be misunderstood and misinterpreted in a Thai context. Some scholars have suggested the practice lacks biblical foundations as well (Bennett, 2011; Chitwood 2001; Dahlfred, 2020; Hulse, 2006).

Definition

According to Bennett (2011), the sinner's prayer is directed to God or Christ and many Christians assume the prayer, if prayed sincerely, will be immediately effective in producing salvation. The prayer typically includes a component of repentance and a request to God for the forgiveness of sins.

Jim Elliff (2021) proposed a harsher definition:

> The typical sinner's prayer as evangelicals have come to express it, has three elements: (1) a mere acknowledgment of sin, which is not the same as repentance, (2) a belief in the act of Christ's death, which is far removed from trust in his person and work, and (3) an "inviting Christ into the life." The last phrase hangs on nothing biblical (though John 1:12 and Revelation 3:20 are used, out of context, for its basis.) It is considered, nonetheless, to be the pivotal and necessary instrument for becoming a true Christian (para 9).

A Short History

Although some believe the sinner's prayer is a biblical practice, the origins of this prayer ritual are relatively recent and can be traced back to American Puritanism and its emphasis on personal religious experience (Leonard, 1985). The individualistic assumptions that undergird the prayer are foreign to the majority world's more collectivist cultures. Large meetings and calls for repentance originated during the Great Awakenings in the United States and England, but the sinner's prayer was unknown to preachers like Wesley, Whitfield, and Edwards. Preaching focused on repentance and a personal reflection on the state of the soul before God (Bennett, 2011, Dahlfred, 2020).

During the Second Great Awakening, Finney and other preachers established the practices of calling people forward, the anxious bench, and the altar call. But those who came forward were counseled and taught, not encouraged to say a ritual prayer. The sinner's prayer was still unknown. Seekers were encouraged to ask God to soften their hearts, to beg God for forgiveness, to ask God to have mercy upon them that he might accept them (Bennett, 2011, pp. 71-75). The onus or burden of salvation rested upon God and not the person saying the prayer. The assumption in these revival meetings was that most people had at least a rudimentary or nominal understanding of God, Christ, and Christianity.

The sinner's prayer ritual did not appear until well into the twentieth century (Chitwood, 2001) with the advent of mass evangelism and a systemized approach to sharing the gospel to large numbers of people. Workers and evangelists were trained in a new method of sharing the gospel and gaining converts. The goal of this new systemized evangelistic process with tracts and standardized presentations focused on encouraging people to say the sinner's prayer, to become "saved" or "born again." The goal is worthy. Many people have made a commitment to follow Jesus through saying a prayer of repentance and dedication to Jesus. However, in Thailand, the context is very different. The level of understanding among the populace is different. Very little is known or understood about repentance, Jesus, or the gospel.

Evidence suggests that the prayer was popularized by Billy Graham and Bill Bright (Chitwood, 2001). Billy Graham's *Steps to Peace with God* and Bill Bright's tract, *the Four Spiritual Laws,* both contain the sinner's prayer at the end of their booklets. The steps to salvation are easily memorized by anyone who wants to "lead someone to the Lord."

Bill Bright admits that his tract has similarities with a sales pitch (Bright, 1985, p. 25). The goal was to lead a person, not to a sale, but to a commitment to follow Jesus. This was an effective methodology in the American cultural context at that time.

However, the culture of the West has changed and the basic knowledge needed to respond to a simple gospel message has decreased. Some Western evangelicals are not supportive of the practice of the sinner's prayer. J.I. Packard declared that the sinner's prayer is a development of "the American production line mentality applied to evangelism" (Chitwood, 2001, p. 69). Leonard (1985) also expressed, "American evangelicals, generally speaking, have moved from an emphasis on conversion experience...to a stress on conversion event - a decisive, often transactional, moment which provides immediate salvation, once and for all" (p. 113). Leonard complains that the focus on the sinner's prayer may place the seeker at the center of the salvation process. Say the prayer sincerely and God is obligated to save. The older model was one of repentance and seeking God's mercy.

Since the mid 20th century, the promotion of the sinner's prayer has spread beyond the United States (Chitwood, 2011). While many people may see the sinner's prayer as their entry point into salvation, and I do not deny that God can use anything to draw people to Him, the prayer has many difficulties and drawbacks, especially in non-Western contexts. The prayer may be acceptable for those who come from at least a nominal Christian background, who have a basic understanding of Jesus and the Christian faith, or who have strayed from the faith into sin. However, in a Buddhist context, few people have any concept of Yahweh or the Messiah who died for our sins. A sermon or simple gospel presentation followed by a prayer may cause more misunderstanding than enlightenment.

Biblical and Theological Problems

Soteriological Assumptions

Salvation is a work of God and is not dependent on human words or actions. As the Apostle Paul wrote, "For by grace you have been saved through faith. And this is not your own doing; it is the gift of God" (Eph. 2:8, ESV). God initiates salvation and God completes the act. For a strict Calvinist, this proposition is axiomatic. God elects those who will be saved and that election is irrevocable. For an Arminian, the action of God is also essential to salvation. "Arminians believe that if a person is saved, it is because God initiated the relationship and enabled the person to respond freely with repentance and faith." (Olsen, 2006, pp. 159-160). From either perspective, God must save us. We cannot earn our salvation and God must open our hearts to Him. The human response to God's grace is faith or trust in the one offering salvation.

Salvation or deliverance from eternal death does not mean there are no consequences for our actions after acknowledging Christ. Scriptures make it clear that we will be judged according to what we have done with what God has provided (Matt. 25:14-30; Luke 19:11-27; 1 Cor. 4:5; 2 Cor. 5:10;1 Pet. 1:17; Revelation 20:12) and some will suffer loss while still being saved (1 Corinthians 3:15). Salvation is passing from death to life, escaping the just penalty for our rebellion against God which is eternal separation from him (2 Thess. 1:9). Salvation is not earned. It is a gift of God, freely given. As the Apostle John wrote, "For God so loved the world, that he gave his only Son, that whoever believes in him should not perish but have eternal life" (John 3:16, ESV). Those who have faith in the Messiah Jesus will not be condemned but pass from death to life.

This salvation is received through faith or by trusting in the Messiah whom God has sent. But salvation requires more than just an acknowledgment of certain facts. Salvation requires a change of allegiance. Matthew Bates (2017) argues that the Greek word for faith pistis (πίστις) is broader than mere belief or assent. The term contains a range of concepts "such as reliability, confidence, assurance, fidelity, faithfulness, commitment, and pledged loyalty" (Bates, 2017, p. 3).

Josephus often used the Greek term pistis to mean allegiance to a king or ruler. (See Josephus, Antiquities 12.47; 12.147; 12.396; Jewish War, 1.207; 2.341). Also, outside the New Testament, the writer of 3 Maccabees uses the term to mean "unswerving loyalty" to the Ptolemaic Dynasty (3 Maccabees 3:3, RSV). Bates argues that translating pistis as allegiance in Paul's letters fits the apostle's understanding of how believers should relate to Jesus.

This grounded understanding of faith (pistis) as allegiance rather than simple belief is a better description of conversion in the Thai context. The call for faith in Jesus is not merely an acceptance of certain theological beliefs or acknowledgement of Jesus as Yahweh God, but a reorientation of allegiance from Buddhism to Christ. Paul's message to the Thessalonian community profoundly reflects the Thai context.

> For not only has the word of the Lord sounded forth from you in Macedonia and Achaia, but your faith in God has gone forth everywhere, so that we need not say anything. 9 For they themselves report concerning us the kind of reception we had among you, and *how you turned to God from idols to serve the living and true God* (1 Thess. 1:8-9, ESV, italics mine).

We might, therefore, paraphrase the passage in Ephesians, "For by grace you have been saved through allegiance, trust, and fidelity to Jesus" (Eph. 2:8). Salvation cannot be reduced to a single prayer. The response is more complex and goes beyond the mere saying of certain words. Salvation is not something that depends on humans and is only observed through an examination of spiritual fruit (Matt. 7:20).

Furthermore, the Great Commission does not call us to make decisions or converts but disciples. "Go therefore and make disciples of all nations, baptizing them in the name of the Father and of the Son and of the Holy Spirit, teaching them to observe all that I have commanded you" (Matt. 28:19-20, ESV). Jesus calls us to lead people into a lifelong journey of learning and growth in relationship with Jesus and His body. In the New Testament, the entry point of that commitment was not prayer, but baptism (Matt. 28:19; Mark 16:16; Acts 2:41; 8:12, 8:36-38, 10:48, 16:31-33, 22:16; Gal. 3:27; Col. 2:12; 1 Peter 3:21).

Baptism indicates incorporation into the body of Christ, spiritually and physically, as part of a community with all its obligations. "For in one Spirit we were all baptized into one body" (1 Corinthians 12:13, ESV). Salvation was not only an individual experience with God but incorporation into the family of God, a communal experience highlighted in baptism and the acceptance of the eucharist or communion. Community and relationships are central to the Thai experience. It is, therefore, all the more important in the Thai context for conversion to be a communal event and not just an individualistic experience, an incorporation into a new family and community.

As the early church grew and moved into a more pagan societal context, repentance, instruction, and an evaluation of life were required before a public proclamation was made in baptism (Canons of Hippolytus, 10-17). Phillip did not hesitate to baptize the Ethiopian eunuch, but the Ethiopian eunuch "had gone to Jerusalem to worship" (Acts 8:27, NIV). The man was a convert to Judaism, or at least a God-fearer, and was well familiar with the Scriptures (Acts 8:26-40). As the church incorporated people from Greek and pagan cultures, more time for instruction was needed. Thai people also have a radically different worldview and need instruction and time to evaluate the claims of Christianity.

A Biblical Examination of the Sinner's Prayer

Several accounts in the Bible have been suggested as types or examples of a sinner's prayer. According to Luke, the thief on the cross declared his trust in Jesus as the Messiah before he died. "Jesus, remember me when you come into your kingdom" (Luke 23:42, ESV). Jesus responded to that expression of allegiance with a promise of entrance into paradise. "Truly, I say to you, today you will be with me in paradise" (Luke 23:43).

Defenders of the sinner's prayer may refer to the Roman Centurion Cornelius who was seeking God in prayer (Acts 10). No sinner's prayer is recorded in this passage, but we know that Cornelius was already a God-fearer, someone who had knowledge of the Torah and had already aligned with Yahweh and the Jewish religion. After hearing the gospel, Cornelius and his whole household accepted the message of the Messiah. They shifted allegiance from the Jewish religion to trust in the Messiah (Acts 10:44-47). The sign that they believed was the "gift of the Holy Spirit" (Acts 10:45, ESV). However, the response to their belief was baptism (Acts 10:47-48).

Peter quotes the Septuagint version of Joel 2:32 on Pentecost, "Everyone who calls upon the name of the Lord shall be saved (Acts 2:21, ESV). However, Peter is not making the point that certain words are salvific or that a prayer must be said. Peter is speaking to Jewish believers in Jerusalem and from the diaspora, urging them to accept the Jewish Messiah. The ritual of allegiance was again baptism (Acts 2:41).

Paul declares, "if you confess with your mouth that Jesus is Lord and believe in your heart that God raised him from the dead, you will be saved" (Romans 10:11, ESV). Surely, this verse is evidence that one must verbally confess trust and allegiance to Jesus. Absolutely! However, Paul is not creating a model for prayer but stating that we must be ready to declare our allegiance to Jesus publicly, perhaps in baptism or as a witness to others. This confession is a brave declaration, especially in a cultural situation where Christians are a minority and where changing one's religion can bring opposition from family and community. My argument is not that the sinner's prayer is not appropriate in some contexts or situations. My argument is that the prayer should not be seen as a portal to salvation. An invitation to discipleship followed by instruction with the goal of public baptism is a more appropriate response to a decision to follow Jesus in the Thai context.

Biblical and Theological Summary

In summary, we have no biblical mandate for encouraging people to say the sinner's prayer. This does not mean that we cannot encourage people to commit to following Jesus through prayer. However, we must not assume that this prayer is salvific. The sinner's prayer ritual comes from an individualistic cultural context that is foreign to Thai culture. The biblical process is to call people into discipleship, learning, and community leading to baptism. Salvation is the work of God. Our job is not to judge who is saved or not saved, our job is to teach, love, and disciple. As the Apostle Paul wrote,

> Therefore, do not pronounce judgment before the time, before the Lord comes, who will bring to light the things now hidden in darkness and will disclose the purposes of the heart. Then each one will receive his commendation from God" (1 Cor. 4:5, ESV).

The responsibility of all Christians is to call the lost to discipleship, baptizing them and teaching them to obey all that Christ taught us (Matt. 28:19-20). The true result will not be seen until the end of time. Those who have persevered to the end are those who will be saved.

And you, who once were alienated and hostile in mind, doing evil

> deeds, [22] he has now reconciled in his body of flesh by his death, in order to present you holy and blameless and above reproach before him, [23] if indeed you continue in the faith (Col 1:21-23, ESV).

> For we have come to share in Christ, if indeed we hold our original confidence firm to the end. (Hebrews 3:14, ESV).

Practical Problems

If the number of hands raised is an indication, thousands are being saved monthly in Thailand. While the number of churches in Thailand is growing, the best statistics indicate that evangelical Christians are still less than one percent of the population (eSTAR Foundation). Counting hands raised and words recited as indications of genuine faith in Christ may be naive if they do not reflect actual church growth.

While Cru has recorded thousands of decisions for Christ over the years, only 3% of those decisions are ever incorporated into a local congregation (Bennett, 2011, loc. 607). Bennett concludes that "it seems highly probable that most of the remaining 97% were not truly converted, and that may also apply even to some of the 3%" (Bennett, 2011, loc 613). Statistics can be misleading, but we must acknowledge that decisions are not a good measure of true conversion. McIntyre (2005) recounts that Billy Graham admitted that the number of actual conversions from his crusades was only around 25% of those who came forward (p. 4).

One should examine research methodology before fully trusting statistical reports. According to McIntyre (2005), 84 to 97% of those who say the sinner's prayer do not continue in the faith (p. 12). Whether these numbers are accurate or not, all reports show that only a small percentage of people who say the sinner's prayer continue to follow Jesus. Some may note that this percentage still represents many people who come to faith in Jesus. That is true. However, my point is that saying the prayer does not immediately translate to incorporation into the body of Christ and discipleship. Furthermore, McIntyre (2005) asserts that "the modern altar call is deceptive if it implies that everyone who comes forward and repeats a formula 'salvation prayer' is saved at that moment" (p. 30).

In 2009, the Billy Graham association sponsored a major evangelistic effort in Thailand called the "My Hope Thailand project." Just before Christmas, a television program was broadcast several times throughout Thailand. The program, recorded on DVD, was also widely distributed to households throughout the kingdom. Over half of all Christian churches in Thailand participated in the three-night event by inviting people to watch the program either on television or on the DVD recording. The program included preaching by Billy and Franklin Graham dubbed into the Thai language. Several well-known Thai celebrities and pop stars gave their testimony. At the end of the program, people were encouraged to decide for Christ and pray the sinner's prayer. Almost 12,000 decisions for Christ were reported.

However, Martin and Visser (2012) reported no significant increase in baptisms or church attendance as a result of the event. The church in Thailand has an annual growth rate of 4%. The growth rate that next year did not increase. A significant amount of money and effort was invested in an event that had no discernable impact on church growth. More than that, according to Martin and Visser (2012), "The strong emphasis on the three nights leading up to a decision was counter-productive" (p. 137). Thai culture is relational. More time is needed for people to examine the claims of Christianity and the people who claim to follow Christ. Expecting Thai people to "make a decision" for Christ based on a recorded sermon by a foreigner is unrealistic.

Many people attend my Thai church for months, often six months to a year, before making a confident decision to follow Christ. In my church, where the sinner's prayer is not encouraged, it is common for a person to join in worship, prayer, small group, and discipleship before finally deciding to become a Christian. During the process, the person may unashamedly say, "I am Buddhist "or "I am Buddhist/Christian." We don't contradict them, at least not directly. That person is "counting the cost," examining the community, and considering the claims of Christ. To encourage such a person to pray a prayer of commitment to Christ before he or she is ready can be harmful to the natural process of coming to an informed and confident commitment to Christ.

According to Jim Elliff, the pattern of the sinner's prayer "has been passed down and repeated because few are taking the necessary time to examine both its flight from scriptural precedent and its dismal effect" (Elliff, 2021). This practice does not work in Thailand and it may not work any longer in the Western context which is drifting from Christian foundations. The Thai church should discard these practices for ones that fit within the Thai cultural context. At the very least, Thai leaders should acknowledge that the sinner's prayer in itself is not salvific. Rather than leading to salvation, promoting the sinner's prayer often leads to problems, disappointment, and confusion.

Cultural Problems

Western culture values individualism and independence while Thailand is a more collectivist culture. Thai people value long-term relationships and commitment to the group. Thai people are, in general, less competitive, and less assertive in relationships than those in the West (Punturaumporn, 2001). Calling for a change of loyalty from one group to another, from the Buddhist community to the Christian community, takes time and patience. Rushing to call for a commitment to a new community runs counter to cultural norms and practices.

The sinner's prayer was developed in an individualistic culture that was, at the time, at least nominally Christian. Most people in Thailand have very little knowledge or experience with Christianity. One member of my church recounted how she heard the gospel for the first time in a university class. The teacher read the portion of scripture where Jesus tells us to turn the other cheek. The whole class laughed. The concept sounded absurd. Many Christian ideas sound absurd to the Buddhist mindset: allegiance to Christ alone, salvation as a free gift that cannot be merited, no cycle of death and rebirth. Thai people have much to understand and process before a commitment can be fully and freely made.

Earlier, I discussed in simplistic terms the concept of krengjai which is "an emotion of deference and avoidance of conflict" (Hilderbrand, 2019, p. 3). This foundational Thai concept is important to understand if one is to communicate the gospel effectively. According to Punturaumporn (2001), "The Thai emphasis on smooth and pleasant interpersonal interactions is closest in meaning to the concept of krengjai" (p. 51). Krengjai is a reticence to bother another person unless it is absolutely necessary (Klausner, 1981). In a study of moral motivation among religiously committed persons (Hilderbrand, 2019), krengjai was found to be a significant factor in Thai moral identity. In other words, violating krengjai in Thai culture can be perceived as disrespectful or even immoral. Therefore, Thai people will often raise their hands and pray the sinner's prayer out of a sense of krengjai or obligation, not sincerity. Encouraging people to pray before that person is ready can be seen as a violation of Thai culture. Furthermore, in an ironic twist, it could be that the Christian church in Thailand has adopted the practice of the sinner's prayer mostly out of krengjai and a sense of obligation to foreign missionaries and teachers.

A common complaint among Thai Buddhists is that Christianity promotes immorality. One can escape karma and punishment by repeating a simple prayer. All sins are forgiven, past and future. No change is needed, Jesus forgives it all. Unfortunately, I find this belief in the Thai Christian community as well. If one says the prayer, all will be forgiven. Sin boldly because Jesus will forgive everything. Without proper instruction, seekers may think that the sinner's prayer is simply a talisman against karma and that sin has no consequences.

Dahlfred (2020), a missionary to Thailand, wrote that encouraging people to say the sinner's prayer can reinforce animistic beliefs. "Though the sinner's prayer is designed to help people become Christians, in many cases it has the opposite effect of confirming people in a fundamentally animistic worldview" (Dahlfred, 2020, p. 7). Thai Buddhism is very animistic with a belief in sacred relics, charms, fortunetelling, and sorcery. The prayer might be seen as a ritual that is required for God to grant the desired wish. In order to receive healing, financial blessing, or other requests, the Christian god appears to require that we first say this ritual prayer. Others may see the prayer as a magical incantation granting blessing. Without a firm understanding of the gospel message, "the words in the sinner's prayer are automatically redefined by the listener to fit their animistic worldview" (Dahlfred, 2020, p. 8).

Solutions

We cannot simply replace the sinner's prayer with baptism. The image of immediate baptism upon belief is found throughout the book of Acts. But the early church quickly began requiring a significant time of training and teaching before baptism was allowed (Canons of Hippolytus, 10-17). People needed to understand the gospel message and have time to count the cost of following Jesus (Luke 14:26-33). For the early church, following Jesus might mean martyrdom. For Thai Buddhists, following Jesus might mean rejection from family and society. For Thai Muslims, who are increasingly coming to Christ, the cost truly could be their life.

In one church that had recently lost its pastor, I was asked to teach a class for baptismal candidates. I was surprised to find that most of the candidates had little to no understanding of Jesus or Christianity. I asked each person, "Who is Jesus?" One person proclaimed boldly that Jesus was the foreigner's god. When I asked why she wanted to join the church, her response was even more surprising. She wanted to join because the church was fun and her friends were Christian. Of the six who were in the class, only one person had an accurate understanding of the gospel that was appropriate for a baptismal candidate.

The Great Commission commands us to make disciples, lifelong followers of the Way, not simply people who have said a prayer. The Jesus model of discipleship is relational. "And he [Jesus] appointed twelve (whom he also named apostles) *so that they might be with him*" (Mark 3:14, ESV, italics mine).

Jesus practiced a relational evangelism. He met with Nicodemus to teach and challenge (John 3). Jesus was not quick to incorporate seekers into his discipleship group. He tested and challenged them to think with his teaching and parables. The rich young ruler (Matt. 19:16-22; Mark 10:17-22; Luke 18:18-23) was seeking eternal life, but Jesus challenged his motivation and dedication. The goal was never to have a large gathering, although large crowds followed Him. The goal was to find those who were committed to the Way and willing to be true disciples.

As I wrote elsewhere:

> Here is the distinction between making converts and making disciples. Conversion has a particular end point. A person crosses over from sinner to saint, unbeliever to believer, unsaved to saved. That is the work of God. I cannot fully discern when that event actually takes place or ever takes place in a particular person. Church attendance is no guarantee of salvation. Only God knows the heart. I certainly do not. My job, discipleship, is the unending process of guiding a person from where they are, saved or unsaved, to a close and personal relationship with God and

> to travel with them in learning everything Christ has commanded us (Hilderbrand, 2021, p. 11)

I do not oppose large churches. Large churches have resources for evangelism and discipleship. Large churches create a significant pool of people from which we can find true disciples. Large churches attract those who are seeking Jesus and are interested in learning more. Large churches have programs that attract people. I support mass media or social media as an evangelistic tool. The message of the gospel must be taught and proclaimed with every tool available to us...videos, movies, YouTube. I support large evangelistic events. These events expose large groups of people to the gospel message.

However, we should not invite people to make a sudden commitment to Jesus through a ritualistic prayer. A prayer does not make someone a Christian. Our purpose should be to follow up on those who are interested in learning more. We must disciple people to the point where we are certain of their commitment to the Way and then baptize them as Jesus commanded. Baptism is still not the end of the process. Discipleship must be a lifelong commitment to teaching, learning, and growing in faith.

The Prayer Challenge

What to do about the sinner's prayer? Prayer should not be discarded, but a ritualistic set of words that can be misinterpreted and misunderstood in the Thai context should be abandoned as a practice in Thai churches.

So, what should we do? Recent research has shown that many if not most Thai people who become Christian make that switch of allegiance because they have had a profound, supernatural encounter with God (Hilderbrand, 2016, 2020, 2021). I have often counseled seekers to ask God to show himself, to prove that he is real and that he cares. "For whoever would draw near to God must believe that he exists and that he rewards those who seek him (Hebrews 11:6, ESV). I have never been disappointed in encouraging people to seek God.

A young Thai woman once asked me how she could know that God was real. I told her to talk to Jesus, "Ask Jesus to show himself real and powerful." She then told me that she wanted to go to a football (soccer) game that evening, but it was sold out. She wanted to know if God could get her tickets. I told her she could ask. It never hurts to ask.

She prayed, went to the game, and received tickets in a very surprising, miraculous way (Hilderbrand, 2021, pp.15-16). A Thai carpenter who was seeking God asked Jesus to heal his hand and it was supernaturally healed as he reached for his hammer. He recounted to me, "When I started to grab the hammer and then began to hammer nails, the swelling disappeared. I shouted to the people in the factory that God is real! This God will be my god for the rest of my life" (Hilderbrand 2020, p.7). I have many such stories from my experience as a missionary and pastor in Thailand. Those who truly seek God will have an encounter with God. At least that has been my experience in Thailand. God desires to show seekers that he is real and more powerful than other spirits, powers, or gods. "For I know that the Lord is great, and that our Lord is above all gods" (Psalm 135:5, ESV).

My solution to the sinner's prayer ritual is to replace it with the prayer challenge. "A prayer challenge is a request for God to show himself, to give a sign or evidence of His power" (Hilderbrand, 2021, p. 15).

A Defense of the Prayer Challenge

Someone might object that we should not put God to the test. Did not Jesus rebuke people for seeking a sign? On the contrary, the whole ministry of Jesus was focused on giving signs of his identity as God and Messiah. The healings and exorcisms were signs of the arrival of God's kingdom in the person of Jesus. When John the Baptist was in prison, he sent messengers to Jesus. He was confused. He needed confirmation that Jesus was the Messiah. In response, Jesus pointed the messengers to "the signs." "Go and tell John what you have seen and heard: the blind receive their sight, the lame walk, lepers are cleansed, and the deaf hear, the dead are raised up, the poor have good news preached to them" (Luke 7:22, RSV).

Jesus rebuked the doubters not because they sought signs, but because they did not believe the signs that were already given. "Truly, truly, I say to you, you are seeking me, not because you saw signs, but because you ate your fill of the loaves" (John 6:26, RSV). Jesus confirms that he gave the people signs, but the people misunderstood or refused to believe those signs. Even when Jesus rebuked people for seeking a sign wrongly, Jesus still promised them one final sign, the resurrection (Matt. 12:38-39; Matt. 16:1-4; Luke 11:29). God does not hesitate to confirm his reality and love to those who seek Him. The author of Hebrews wrote, "This salvation, which was first announced by the Lord, was confirmed to us by those who heard him. God also testified to it by signs, wonders and various miracles" (Heb. 2:3-4, NIV).

One might think that a prayer challenge is testing or tempting God. I am not suggesting that we tempt God. We must understand how the words, "to test" or "to tempt." are used in the context of the Scriptures. God commands us to test Him in the book of Malachi. "'Test me in this,'" says the Lord Almighty" (Malachi 3:10, NIV). In the book of Psalms, we are told to "Taste and see that the Lord is good" (Psalms 34:8, NIV). Testing is not always a bad thing. What we are not to test is God's patience (Deuteronomy 6:16), and we are not to solicit God to do something that is against His Will or character (Matthew 4:5-10; Luke 4:1-12). King Hezekiah asked God for a sign that he would be healed, and God sent him a sign (Isaiah 38:22). Gideon humbly asked for confirmation that it was really Yahweh speaking to him and God answered his request (Judges 6:17).

Thai people must be convinced that Jesus is the supreme God who cares for us and is worthy of our allegiance. Thai people need to have an experience with God to be convinced that Yahweh Jesus is God above all other gods. We cannot force this encounter.

Our task is to tell people about Jesus and invite them to ask Jesus to make himself real. Invite God, in his own way, to reveal himself so seekers might know Jesus is real and wants a relationship with them. We trust God to answer in his own way while we continue to teach, disciple, and pray for those who are interested to learn. But we must trust that God wants to reveal himself. I believe He does.

> You will seek me and find me, when you seek me with all your heart (Jer. 29:13, NIV).
> Seek, and you will find (Matt, 7:7, ESV)

Adopting this model may mean our "decision" numbers decrease, but we should focus instead on the number of people we are actively discipling. We should report those numbers or count responses to the prayer challenge. We might also report the number of people we are baptizing. These numbers are more accurate reflections of what God is doing in our midst.

Practical Steps

Practically, in church or in a large meeting, we should invite people to meet and pray with us after service. Train workers to pray for material needs, and for physical, emotional, and spiritual healing. Train workers to pray that the seeker would encounter God in a personal and significant way. Train workers to counsel and help people find a discipleship group where they can learn more and have a relationship with the body of Christ. We must help the seeker process their experiences and what they are learning in light of a Biblical worldview. Only after evidence of true understanding and commitment should we allow people to be baptized. Not every seeker will truly seek. Not every enquirer will follow through. Evangelism is the work of God, but we can point the way.

References

Bates, M. W. (2017). Salvation by allegiance alone: Rethinking faith, works, and the gospel of Jesus the King, Baker Academic.

Bennett, D. (2011). The sinner's prayer: its origins and dangers. Even Before Publishing. Kindle Edition.

Bradshaw, P. F., & Bebawi, C. (2010). The canons of Hippolytus. Gorgias Press.

Bright, B. (1985). Come help change the world. Here's Life Publishers.

Chitwood, P. H. (2001). The sinner's prayer: An historical and theological analysis. PhD Dissertation, The Southern Baptist Theological Seminary. http://hdl.handle.net/10392/4153

Dahlfred, K. (2020). The sinner's prayer in animistic cultures: Problems and solutions. Mission Round Table, 15(1), pp. 4–11.

Elliff, J. (2021). Closing with Christ. In Gospel-centered resources from Midwestern Seminary. https://ftc.co/resource-library/blog-entries/closing-with-christ/
eSTAR Foundation (2021). https://www.estar.ws.
Hilderbrand, K. M. (2016). What led Thai Buddhist background believers to become Christians: A study of one church in Bangkok. Missiology: An International Review, 44(4), pp. 400–415. https://doi.org/10.1177/0091829616666511
Hilderbrand, K. M. (2019). Religio-cultural factors as moral motivation among religiously committed Thai people: a grounded theory study, Journal of Beliefs & Values, 41(1), pp. 5-19. https://doi.org/10.1080/13617672.2019.1584934
Hilderbrand, K. M. (2020). What led Thai Buddhist background believers to become Christian: A grounded theory study, Missiology: An International Review, 48(3), pp. 1-14. https://doi.org/10.1177/0091829620937406
Hilderbrand, K. M. (2021). God the evangelist: Partnering with God in making disciples. Application and commentary on research into the reasons Thai Theravada Buddhists became Christian. BaanRao Publishing.
Hulse, E. (2006). The great invitation: Examining the use of the altar call in evangelism. Audubon Press.
Josephus, F. (2019). Complete works of Josephus: Antiquities of the Jews, The wars of the Jews against Apion, etc. Forgotten Books.
Klausner, J. W. (1981). Reflections on Thai culture: Collected writings of William J. Klausner. Bangkok: Suksit Siam.
Leonard, B. J. (1985). Getting saved in America: Conversion event in a pluralistic culture, Review and Expositor. 82(1), pp. 111-127.
Martin, D., & Visser, M. (2012). Sense and nonsense of large-scale evangelism, Evangelical Missions Quarterly 48(2), pp. 136–137.
McIntyre, P. (2005). The Graham formula: Why most decisions for Christ are ineffective. White Harvest Publications.
Murray, I. H. (1973). The invitation system. Banner of Truth Trust.
Olsen, R. E. (2006). Arminian Theology: Myths and Realities. IVP Press.
Punturaumporn, B. (2001). The Thai style of negotiation: Kreng jai, bunkhun, and other socio-cultural keys to business negotiation in Thailand. Doctoral dissertation. Ohio University.

About the Author

Kelly Michael Hilderbrand, PhD, DMin, is a faculty member and researcher at Bangkok Bible Seminary. He has graduate degrees from Biola University and Fuller Theological Seminary. He is the founding pastor of Our Home Chapel, Bangkok, and the co-founder of a Thai Foundation that supports the education of children at risk.

GREAT COMMISSION
RESEARCH JOURNAL
2022, Vol. 14(1) 87-94

Leadership: Essential for a Church to Grow Numerically and Spiritually

Steven L. Estes

Abstract

This article relates the spiritual gift of leadership (Rom. 12:8) to numerical church growth. Scripture presents spiritually gifted leaders as those who received authority from God and had knowledge of his will for his people. Biblical leaders delegated effectively and encouraged those who were given tasks to accomplish. The overall scope of biblical teaching on leadership indicates that pastors/elders should have the gift of leadership. Allowing those who qualify and have the gift of leadership to emerge is crucial for the health of a church.

My family and I were immediately impressed as we drove into the church parking lot. The whole area seemed like a beehive of activity. There were uniformed helpers directing traffic. People were walking quickly toward the sanctuary. Those still in their cars, including us, were looking in all directions for a place to park. When we entered the church building our first impression was that we were part of something alive, a church that is moving forward. The worship was exciting and far from boring. Then the pastor came forward and began his sermon. Soon it was evident that this preacher had charisma accompanied by tremendous stage presence. But what was even more impressive was that he was gifted for leadership. God had given him authority to shepherd the flock and he cowered before no one. This is a church in the

United States.

Another church I visited was quite different. There was no parking lot and the building was on a dirt road. While the sanctuary was fairly large, it could only be described as rustic. The believers were very friendly and there was a sense of optimism among them. The worship was also quite lively and nothing about it seemed routine. When the pastor stood to speak, he did not appear to be an especially imposing figure. But as his voice rang through the meeting hall, there was again the sense that this preacher was a Spirit-gifted leader. He clearly expected total dedication to Christ from the church members. Anything less was not worthy of our Lord. The sermon cast a vision of hundreds in the area coming to Christ through the church's ministry. Finally, he brought the message to a crescendo by proclaiming, "This city is ours!" This is a church in Northern Argentina.

These two churches illustrate what I believe to be the main impetus to numerical church growth. Most everyone involved in missions has likely heard at least one "key" to church growth and I confess that the following pages offer another. What emboldens me to continue is that, first of all, I believe this key has biblical support, as the many Scripture references will hopefully demonstrate. Secondly, my observations, while limited, have repeatedly confirmed what it is that makes a church grow in numbers.

The Authority of Those with the Spiritual Gift of Leadership

In Romans 12:6, the Apostle Paul begins a list of spiritual gifts. Verse 8 indicates that there is a gift of leadership and those who have it are to "govern diligently." Paul writes to the Thessalonians saying that they are to "respect those who are over you in the Lord and admonish you" (1 Th. 5:12), adding that they should be held in the highest regard (1 Th. 5:13). According to 1 Timothy 5:17, the elders are to "direct the affairs of the church." When addressing elders (Acts 20:17) Paul says they are overseers who are to shepherd the flock of God over which the Holy Spirit has placed them. The elders are to keep watch over "all the flock" (Acts 20:28). In 2 Corinthians Paul explains that God gives authority to leaders to correct and edify (2 Cor. 10:1-2, 6, 8; 13:10) 1 Timothy 3:1-5 teaches that elders are to take care of the flock of God. Similarly, the Apostle Peter writes that elders are to shepherd the flock of God over which the Lord has made them overseers. While elders are not to lord it over the church members, the latter have been entrusted to their care (1 Pet. 5:1-3). The writer to the Hebrews teaches that leaders must be obeyed, and their authority recognized. It is their responsibility to watch over the believers (13:17).

Clearly, some people have the function and gifting for church leadership. These officials would be the elders. It would seem that "elder" is another term for pastor and that such an official must have the gift of leadership. A pastor or shepherd, by definition, leads the sheep. The word "pastor" and references to a pastoral function imply authority for leadership.

We can conclude, therefore, that those with the spiritual gift of leadership have received authority from God to guide and watch over the church. C. Peter Wagner (1994) says that one prerequisite for a church to grow is that the pastor must have the gift of leadership. But the Scriptures above would lead one to question if anyone should be a pastor who doesn't have the gift of leadership. Pastoring and leading are inseparable. As Alexander Strauch points out, pastors must govern, give direction, and provide leadership for the church (Strauch, 2001).

There is much more in the Bible about leadership, including much in the Old Testament. The objection could be raised, however, that no spiritual gift of leadership was mentioned before the Pauline epistles. While there is a sense in which I concede the point, it is also true that what was written before was for our instruction (Rom. 15:4). Old Testament leaders provide biblical examples that can therefore be used as illustrations of how the gift of leadership plays out.

The authority of Moses is especially instructive. Exodus 14:31 says that the people put their trust in the Lord and in Moses after the miracle of crossing the Red Sea. According to Exodus 19:9, the Lord spoke to Moses so the people would always put their trust in Moses. In Numbers 16 we read about the rebellion against Moses led by Korah, Dathan, and Abiram (16:1-2). Moses explains that the people would know that the Lord had sent him to do all he did if the earth swallowed the rebels, and that is what happened (16:28-33). The authority of Moses was transferred to his successor Joshua through the laying on of hands (Num. 27:18-20, 23). Joshua also was filled with a spirit of wisdom because Moses had laid his hands on him. As a result, the Israelites listened to all that Joshua said (Dt. 34:9).

The Lord confirmed the authority of Joshua and other Old Testament leaders as well. He exulted him in the sight of Israel so the people would know that God was with Joshua (Josh. 3:7; 4:14). When Samuel prayed, the Lord caused thunder and rain, which resulted in the people being in awe of Samuel and the Lord (1 Sam. 12:18). The Lord exulted King Solomon and clothed his reign with magnificence (1 Ch. 29:25).

All this is not to say that spiritual leaders are immune from opposition, as is illustrated by the rebellion of Korah, Dathan, and Abiram (Num. 16:1-2). In fact, the congregation criticized Moses and assembled against him in the same chapter (Num. 16:41-42). There are other examples of conflict in the life of Moses. The people complained that he had brought them out of Egypt to have them killed and they wanted to replace him with another leader (Ex. 14:10-12; Num. 14:2-4). More than once the entire community complained against Moses because of a lack of water (Ex. 15:24; 17:1-3). They also took him to task because of the food they ate during their journey (Nu. 11:4-6; 21:4-5). As Aaron

Wildavsky (1984) points out, Moses faced opposition during his entire career as a leader. However, God sent a plague, which resulted in the death of 14,700 people, and caused Aaron's rod to sprout in order to affirm Moses' leadership (Nu. 16: 46-49; 17:1-10). In other words, conflict does not necessarily destroy a leader's ministry and, over the long haul, may not impede numerical growth in a church led by spiritually gifted leaders.

Spiritual authority from God is a characteristic of biblical leaders. While the gift of leadership did not appear until the New Testament, in the Old Testament, leaders were endowed with authority for leadership, although opposition to their authority was not unknown. This biblical pattern has strong implications for pastors. Only those gifted for leadership are going to have an effective pastoral ministry.

Leaders Have Clear Direction from the Lord

In Scripture, leaders often had clear direction from the Lord as to his will for his people. For example, God revealed to Moses that he was going to free the Hebrew slaves from the Egyptians and lead them to the Promised Land (Ex. 6:2, 6-8). The Lord specifically told Joshua that he would lead the Israelites into the Promised Land and they would take control of it (Jos. 1:1-4, 6). It was also Joshua whom God clearly led to confront and defeat the armies of Ai and the Amorite kings (Jos. 8:1-2; 10:6-8). In 1 Chronicles 14:8-16, King David twice asked for God's direction when he led his men into battle with the Philistines, and God answered with specific instructions.

Sometimes God gave direction to a leader indirectly. The Lord communicated through Shemaiah to King Rehoboam that he should not attack his fellow Israelites (2 Ch. 11:1-4). King Jehoshaphat consulted the Lord when a great multitude gathered against him. In response, the Spirit of the Lord gave guidance through Jahaziel, and Judah was delivered (2 Ch. 20:2-3, 14-22). When the Assyrians threatened Jerusalem, King Hezekiah prayed to the Lord, pleading for help. God answered through the prophet Isaiah indicating that the Assyrians would not be able to attack the city (Isa. 37:1, 15, 20-21, 32-35). Zerubbabel discovered that his job was to lead the people in rebuilding the temple because of God's revelation through the prophets Haggai (Hag. 1:1-4, 8, 12-14; 2:1, 4, 9) and Zechariah (Zec. 4:6, 9).

It makes sense that those to whom the Lord gives authority for leadership will know His will for those whom they are to lead. When pastors have a clear sense of God's leading, churches tend to be healthier as they move toward a divinely inspired goal. Such a goal unites the church and motivates the members to action. At the same time, knowing what God is *not* leading a church to do prevents a lot of wasted time and energy on ministries that are not fruitful. Churches without a leader who is convinced of God's will for the congregation tend to flounder and not accomplish much.

Leaders Delegate

Someone has said followers like to do things, while leaders like to get others to do things. It is indeed interesting how many times in the Bible a leader delegated tasks to others. Moses appointed judges to settle disputes so that he would not have to resolve all of them himself (Ex. 18:13-26). The Levites were instructed by Moses to place the Book of the Law next to the Ark of the Covenant as a witness against Israel (Dt. 31:24-26). We find that twice Joshua sent men to check out enemy territory before the soldiers attacked (Jos. 2:1, 7:2). He also had three representatives of each tribe survey, describe, and divide into sections much of Israel after the conquest (Jos.18:1-6, 8). Jehoida the priest placed the Levitical priests and gatekeepers to serve in the temple (2 Ch. 23:14, 18-19). Nehemiah put men in charge of distributing supplies to the priests and Levites (Ne. 13:13). Hanani and Hananiah were told by Nehemiah to select people to be guards in Jerusalem after the wall was completed (Ne. 7:1-3). Nehemiah also assigned gatekeepers to patrol the night before the Sabbath (Ne. 13:19, 22). Our Lord delegated the task of world evangelization to his followers (Mt. 4:19; 28:18-20; Acts 1:8).

There are several examples of when Old Testament kings were involved in delegating tasks to others. Pharaoh turned over to Joseph the leadership and administration of all of Egypt (Gen. 41:39-41). David and Samuel assigned gatekeepers for the tabernacle (1 Ch. 9:22-23). King David delegated offering sacrifices, guarding the gates, and giving thanks to the Lord (1 Ch. 16:37-41). Officials were named by David to be in charge of secular and sacred matters among the Transjordanian tribes (1 Ch. 26:32). King Solomon and the priest Jehoiada made similar assignments for various responsibilities (2 Ch. 8:12, 14; 23:18-19). Solomon appointed men to build the temple and the King's palace. Leaders were also appointed as supervisors to make sure the construction work went forward (2 Ch. 2:1-2, 17-18). Jehoshaphat sent officials to teach the people God's law (2 Ch. 17:5, 7-9). He also appointed judges and priests to settle disputes. Over them, Amariah the chief priest was to be responsible for spiritual matters, and Zebadiah was to be in charge of royal issues (2 Ch. 19:5-11). King Joash commanded that the Levites be in charge of collecting the annual offering prescribed by Moses. Joash asked the chief priest Jehoiada why the Levites did not collect the offering, implying that Jehoiada was put in charge of administering the collection (2 Ch. 24:1, 5-6). Both of them hired carpenters and masons to work on the restoration of the temple (2 Ch. 24:11-12). The Levites were assigned the task of purifying the temple through King Hezekiah (2 Ch. 29:1, 4-5). Hezekiah also sent couriers with letters inviting the people of Judah and Israel to the Passover celebration (2 Ch. 30:1, 6). Hezekiah organized the Levites and priests for their duties of offering burnt sacrifices and singing praises. He also appointed Levites and priests to distribute the monetary contributions received to their fellow Levites and priests (2 Ch. 31:2, 13-20). Storerooms were prepared at the order of Hezekiah for the offerings received for the priests and Levites (2 Ch. 31:4, 9-11). King Josiah delegated repairing the temple to other people (2 Ch. 34:8). He also delegated to the priests and Levites the celebration of the Passover (2 Ch. 35:1-6, 16). In still another case King Artaxerxes delegated to Ezra the Priest the job of investigating the spiritual condition of Judah. Then the king commanded Ezra to delegate the task of administering justice in Trans-Euphrates to magistrates, whom he was to appoint (Ezra 7:12, 14, 25).

Clearly, there are many times when a biblical leader delegated an important task. At first glance, getting others to do things may sound like laziness on the part of leaders. But the reality is that much more gets done when leaders delegate effectively. One pastor assigned jobs to those that faithfully attended his men's Bible study. Other factors contributed, but afterward, the church began to grow impressively. Biblical leaders have a clear sense of God's will for the group and passionately seek to raise up those who will work towards attaining a divinely revealed goal.

Leaders Encourage

Since leaders delegate, it follows that they will seek to inspire those to whom they have given an important task. Both the American pastor and the Argentine pastor mentioned earlier do this very effectively. Another attribute of leaders is that they encourage others. While that is not always the case (e.g., Dt. 9:6-8, 16, 22-24; 31:24-29), there are numerous examples in Scripture of leaders offering encouragement. When the Egyptians trapped the Israelites at the edge of the Red Sea, Moses told them not to be afraid because God was going to deliver them from harm and fight the battle for them against their enemy (Ex. 14:13-14). Moses was to encourage Joshua because he would conquer the land. He also explained that the Lord was going to fight for Joshua during the conquest (Dt. 1:1, 37-38; 3:21-22). Joshua told the people to consecrate themselves because the following day God was going to do wonders among them, which occurred when they crossed the Jordan River (Jos. 3:5, 14-16). After circling Jericho seven times, Joshua told the Israelites to shout because God had given them the city and they would conquer it (Jos. 6:2, 16-17). Ehud rallied the Israelites against Moab, proclaiming that God had delivered the Moabites into their hands (Jdg. 3:26-28).

Nehemiah gave a pep talk to the men who were with him so they would start rebuilding the wall of Jerusalem (Ne. 1:1, 2:12, 17-18). Nehemiah told the leaders and the people not to fear the enemy because God is great in power. He added that God was going to fight for them and they should defend their families and homes (Ne. 4:13-14, 20). In Nehemiah 9:5, the Levites exhorted the people to praise God for his greatness. Through a prophecy, Azariah encouraged King Asa to follow the Lord (2 Ch. 15:1-2, 7-8, 16).

Jesus encouraged the disciples by saying that He had all authority in heaven and earth and that He would always be with them. Our Savior further explained that the Holy Spirit would come upon them, giving power for the task of bearing witness (Mt. 28:18-20; Ac. 1:8). In Acts 14:22, Paul and Barnabas encouraged followers of Jesus to remain steadfast in their faith.

Just as Old Testament Kings delegated, they also repeatedly encouraged. David pointed out to Solomon all the provisions he had made for the building of the temple. Abundant supplies and workers were available. On that basis, David encouraged him to get on with the job (1 Ch. 22:7, 14, 15-16). David added that God was with Solomon, and he could count on God's presence until the temple was completed (1 Ch. 28:10, 20). Jehoshaphat appointed people to settle disputes in Israel and encouraged them to be courageous as they carried out their duties (2 Ch. 19:8-9, 11). "Hezekiah spoke encouragingly to all the Levites" (2 Ch. 30:22). King Hezekiah told the people not to fear the Assyrians because God was greater than the enemy and would fight the battle for Judah (2 Ch. 32:6-8). We read that "the people gained confidence from what Hezekiah the king of Judah said" (2 Ch. 32:8). Josiah encouraged the priests and Levites in their service for the temple, the Lord, and all Israel (2 Ch. 35:1-3).

There is a good reason for the many cases in Scripture where leaders encouraged others. They are included because it is important to do so! The many examples one finds also imply that followers tend to get discouraged. Pastors who are adept at lifting the spirits of others have a great advantage as they seek to take a church forward.

Conclusion

Romans 12:8 instructs those with the spiritual gift of leadership to govern diligently. Those who are so gifted have received authority from God to guide and watch over the church, even though such gifting does not exempt leaders from opposition. Looking at examples of biblical leaders leads us also to conclude that those with the spiritual gift of leadership have a clear sense of God's will for the group, an ability to delegate effectively, and a tendency to encourage others. My observation is that, in Argentina and the United States, a church grows when the pastor has the spiritual gift of leadership, that is to say, when the pastor is clearly a leader. Certainly, there are other pastoral attributes, such as effective preaching and teaching (1 Ti. 3:2; 5:17), that contribute to the numerical growth of the church. But it is not hard to imagine that a church would grow if the pastor had authority from the Lord, knowledge of God's leading, the capacity to mobilize others, and the ability to inspire followers toward the goals God has for the church. The two pastors I mentioned at the outset are prime examples of gifted leaders of growing churches.

There are other crucial requirements in the Bible for spiritual leaders (1 Ti. 3:1-7; Tit. 1:5-9). Paul directed Titus to appoint elders in every town, listing the requirements that are necessary for becoming an elder (Tit. 1:5). Paul and Barnabas named elders in the churches of Lystra, Iconium, and Antioch (Acts 14:21, 23) even though these were new churches (Strauch, 2001). But, as we saw earlier, those who are elders/pastors must have the spiritual gift of leadership in order to carry out their ministry effectively.

How does the existence of people who meet the qualifications for elder/pastor apply to numerical church growth? If a church is not growing should the pastor resign so that someone with the gift of leadership can emerge? Of course, that cannot be a hard and fast rule for every situation. Some churches would sink into severe problems or even dissolve if the pastor were suddenly to resign. In other situations, a church might not grow even with spiritually gifted leadership (e.g., a congregation of exclusively elderly people in a region of mainly young families). But, as a general rule, would the resignation of the pastor in a non-growing church be advisable? I submit that the key to numerical church growth is allowing those with the gift of leadership, and who meet the other Scriptural requirements, to pastor churches.

References

Strauch, A. (2001). Liderazco Bíblico de Anicianos: Un Urgente Llamado a Restaurar el Liderazgo Bíblico en las Iglesias. Lewis and Roth Publishers.

Wagner, C. P. (1994). Your Spiritual Gifts Can Help Your Church Grow (Revised). Regal Books.

Wildavsky, A. (1984). The Nursing Father: Moses as a Political Leader. University of Alabama Press.

About the Author

Steven L. Estes (D.Miss.) served as a missionary to Argentina for 35 years. Estes taught at the Seminario Bautista Evangélico Argentina and worked in church planting.

GREAT COMMISSION
RESEARCH JOURNAL
2022, Vol. 14(1) 95-100

My Journey in Church Growth

Bob Orr

At the request of my good friend Gary McIntosh, I am going to recount my more than 40-year journey in the field of Church Growth.

The Beginning Years

In 1970, as a young seminary graduate, I was called to my first pastorate: a German-speaking Baptist Church trying to become an English-speaking church in a community experiencing a vast influx of Portuguese immigrants. I knew nothing more than the mandate to make disciples was real and that no excuses were allowed.

In seeking to figure how to be faithful to our mandate to disciple *panta ta enthne*, I tried a few things, some that were successful, and others that lie on the scrapheap of history.

Two things worked well. The first was learning how to attract and pastor the unchurched. Within a couple of years, I had a parish of over 150 people who were unchurched and unreached in our community. As the relationships developed, many of them came to faith in Christ. The strategy was simple: I went door to door asking people if they attended church. If they said yes, I asked if I could pray a prayer of blessing on them. If they said no, I asked if they could ever imagine a time when they might need a pastor they could call upon and count on. If they could envision that, I asked them, with no obligation, if I could be their pastor. We would exchange numbers and I would call them once a month to see how they were doing and pray with them about anything going on in their lives. I remembered the words of Jesus about sheep in search of a shepherd.

The second thing that worked well was recognizing that everybody knows somebody. Using the existing relationships we have is an important way to take seriously our mandate. The church truly does grow through whom the members know. We had a significant number of nurses and doctors in our church who were German and worked at the largest general hospital in the city that was less than 100 yards away. Before long, we started to see a stream of nursing students, and medical personnel who came, not because the church was English speaking or had a German heritage, but because their friends invited them. The same pattern happened with schoolteachers and independent contractors.

I eventually wrote about both of these concepts for articles in the early issues of the magazine *Church Growth: America.* I believe one of them ended up in the first edition of *The Pastor's Church Growth Handbook*, edited by Win Arn in 1979.

I give this short background to tell you about a critical experience in 1973 when my denomination, the North American Baptist Conference in Western Canada, was holding its annual pastors' conference at the Banff Springs Hotel. The guest presenters at that time were Dr. Donald McGavran and his protégé Win Arn who had recently launched the Institute for American Church Growth. Not only was I fascinated listening to them, but I also gained a theoretical framework to understand some of the things I had been doing.

At that conference, I had been asked to lead a workshop. To my surprise, both Dr. McGavran and Dr. Arn were in the audience. After I finished my presentation, McGavran and Arn came up to talk to me. McGavran asked me about visiting my church and told Arn that he needed to come too.

The following year, Arn conducted this Basic Church Growth Seminar, which was relatively new, at our church and several other locations around our province. As Arn's host, the extended one-on-one time together created a life-long friendship that resulted in our working together for most of my ministry.

A year later, Arn hosted his First Advanced Church Growth Seminar for pastors in Pasadena, California. He invited me to come and present. I had no idea what I was getting into. At that conference, the speakers included not only Win Arn, but also Lyle Schaller, Bob Schuller, Dr. Paul David Cho, Ted Engstrom, Art Glasser, Peter Wagner, and the father of the movement Dr. McGavran himself. Each of these men became a friend. What they have done for Christ and His kingdom is nothing short of amazing.

When the conference was over, Arn invited me to meet with Dr. McGavran and himself. He asked me if I would be willing to be a consultant and seminar leader for the Institute for American Church Growth. As far as I know, I was the first of these leaders. I not only went home to Canada and began helping scores of Churches, but I also started getting regular calls from Pasadena from Arn asking me if I could go somewhere on such and such a date and conduct a seminar on behalf of the Institute. I found myself doing 25-30 of these conferences each year.

The Second Phase

Eventually, pastoring a church, teaching at the local Bible College, and doing the seminars made it so that I had too much on my plate. I had to ask myself, "What does my future look like? Where does God want me to serve?" After prayer, discussion with my family, and the counsel of my spiritual advisors, I resigned from my church and formed the Institute for Canadian Church Growth. I was now devoted full time to this fledgling discipline. My schedule quickly filled up and I found myself traveling to every province in Canada serving as a consultant for over a dozen denominations and conducting seminars on Church Growth for congregations in Canada. I was grateful for the help and resources given to me by McGavran and Arn. I was still traveling for Arn to many places in the United States; my time was spent equally between the two countries.

1982-1983

In December of 1982, Arn asked me to join him for a conference in Chicago. When it was over, he asked me if I would consider combining our two organizations in Pasadena to take Church Growth principles across not only the States and Canada but to wherever God would open up the doors. After going through the requisite immigration hoops, our family moved to Pasadena in a U-Haul. We arrived in mid-August and by the beginning of September, I found myself someplace (and sometimes in more than one place) every week, helping churches put into practice Church Growth principles.

The Institute Years 1983 -1994

These years were filled with travel to 48 countries, work with 56 denominations, and seminars or consultations in over 3000 churches. I was on the road about 200 days a year and have the dubious distinction of being the first person in history to have traveled 1,000,000 miles on Northwest Airline domestic routes.

The creative whirlwind at the Institute during those years saw Church Growth as a discipline come of age. Here are a few highlights.

Church growth became a holistic discipline with seminars on topics such as Sunday School, Assimilation, Lay Ministry, Oikos Evangelism, and Worship that Attracts and Holds the Unchurched. I had a large part to play in writing the curriculum for some of the seminars, including Assimilation, Lay Ministry, Faith Planning, 25 Ways to Reach The Unchurched, Worship, and a specialty conference for small churches. The manuals for some of these seminars were used by the Cumberland Presbyterians as well as other denominations.

During this time, we designed specialized training for Pastors Conferences. Often, we would receive a call from a group of pastors or denominational executives and customize the material for the group. I remember a lecture that outlined the DNA of a growing church that was so well received and relevant that some younger consultants such as Chad Thibodaux used it as the basis of a method to determine a church's health. It can be found on my blog (http://drboborr.blogspot.com/) under the title "The Ethos of a Growing Church."

These seminars led to the development of a 2-year plan for a regional judicatory or a local church. We would visit the churches every 4-6 months, providing training and consulting to help them become more growth-oriented. It was during this period that my friend Dr. Gary McIntosh joined the organization to help pastors and churches collect the information needed to apply for this 2-year plan.

Perhaps the best conference or training we offered was our Diagnose and Renew Your Church conference. We developed an 85-page diagnostic tool that covered every aspect of church life. I wrote the first draft of the diagnostic tool and then Charles Arn and I worked together to refine it. After a church completed as much of the diagnostic tool as it could, we would spend 3 days going through the data and discussing what it meant. Many parts of this diagnostic tool are still being used. I was the lead presenter and often had Win Arn, Charles Arn, Gary McIntosh, Steve Wagner, or Bob Bast with me as co-presenters. Occasionally, I led all 3 days myself. I do not have the fondest memories of such seminars because presenting morning, afternoon, and evening sessions took an unbelievable amount of energy to keep the participants engaged. As I look back on this conference, however, it allowed churches to get 80% of the benefits of a two-person conference without paying for a second consultant. This probably helped thousands of small- and medium-sized churches.

During this time, we also focused on training consultants whom we called Church Growth Associates. Hundreds of pastors and denominational executives came to the Institute for training and resources so that they could take Church Growth principles to their areas of ministry.

We also trained chaplains for the United States Navy. I remember two officers from the Navy coming to Pasadena to meet with us. We appropriately adapted the seminar and had the privilege of going to 25 bases around the world to train chaplains in outreach. We also developed a second conference on worship in the Navy. I am still friends with many of these chaplains.

As the Church Growth seminars became better known, I found myself in Japan, China, India, Malaysia, New Zealand, Australia, and numerous other countries teaching Church Growth principles to pastors and lay leaders.

The Following Years

Although Dr. Arn had a stroke, he was still a vibrant and brilliant Church Growth expert. He changed his research focus toward reaching people neglected by most churches. I found myself wondering how my life would change as activity at the Institute was winding down.

Church Growth had changed and our seminars in many respects had been replaced by the megachurch conferences led by practitioners of the discipline.

Pastors such as Rick Warren and Bill Hybels were drawing thousands of pastors to "See how to do it" seminars held on their campuses, The number of National Church Growth Conferences dropped accordingly.

I formed a new company called Growth Associates and began a time of seeking to understand how I could most effectively use what I had learned. I entered back into the pastorate, the real laboratory for what we had been teaching. Not to my surprise, I found these principles really did work. McGavran's mantra rang in my head: There was more indifference to the gospel in a church than in the surrounding community. I truly did find in the community a vast mosaic of people who could be reached with the gospel.

My "expertise" still gave me opportunities to keep my heart and hands in the discipline. I conducted a study, at the invitation of Carlise Driggers and Bill Mackey of the Baptist Convention of South Carolina, that received an award for Religious research on the subject of values and their influence on church growth. The South Carolina Baptist Convention was a cutting-edge group that included such people as Bobby Jackson, George Bullard, and Reggie McNeil. To this day, the time and effort I invested in that region are still discussed. The Lilly Foundation printed the summary report entitled "Values for Growing Churches" and sent it to 40,000 churches. (The report can be found at http://drboborr.blogspot.com/2012/02/values-for-growing-churches.html)

I had the privilege of working with my denomination, the North American Baptist Conference in Western Canada, on numerous programs including Church Revitalization, Breaking the 200 Barrier, Helping the Small Church Grow, and other activities for which the leaders felt my expertise was relevant.

My work continued to take me overseas regularly with 4 trips to India, 3 to Korea, 14 to New Zealand, 6 to Australia, 3 to Brazil, and 2 to Africa. These trips involved primarily pastoral conferences or Bible college classes. During these trips, I had the privilege of meeting many Church Growth leaders including Yonggi Cho, George Mabeleo, Ken Henson, Jeff and Becky Hrubrik, and Ray Muller. The list could go on but suffice it to say I have been greatly enriched by whom I have met; the contribution I made seems so small in comparison.

One of my great privileges during the last years of their lives was my regular times with my friends Donald McGavran and Win Arn. As Arn's health began to fail, our twice a month visits typically focused on recounting stories about pastors and churches we had visited. Our times were especially meaningful when we remembered the stories of lives that had been changed. Arn had a phenomenal impact on my life and ministry; I still love to discuss with all who ask about him his passion for the local church. I especially remember watching Win shed tears of joy when he heard of someone coming to faith in Christ as a result of the effort he had put into training and investing in people's lives.

I also regularly visited McGavran during the final years of his life. I had the privilege of presenting the final set of lectures he gave before his passing (by reading them aloud for him) in North Carolina. I have been digitizing the original manuscripts and putting them on my blog. I have also published them in a book called *The Final Lectures*. There is a tribute to McGavran on my blog and you can read about it there. The last words he spoke to me were the same as his first words at the first conference I attended back in 1973, "It's God's will that his church grow and that his lost children be found."

Currently, I am the president of California State Christian University. It is a new kind of seminary that adopted two of McGavran's ideas and has made them part of the school's DNA. First, all of our faculty are successful practitioners who are not only academically qualified but also have practical ministry experience and know-how to apply biblical truth in context. As someone remarked, "Your professors play with real bullets." Second, we require a course in evangelism, church growth, and missiology every quarter. We also require every student, regardless of major, to participate in an overseas mission trip to understand where and how God is at work. We believe every Christian leader needs to have the passion and expertise necessary for leading churches in fulfilling our Lord's commands.

I still speak at a limited number of Church Growth Conferences around the world as well as doing local church consultations. As I reflect on my life, I have been changed. But the main thing is still the main thing: We serve a God who loves to see lost people found and the mandate to make disciples is still binding on each and every one of us till he returns.

I would say to those who follow after me that the principles of Church Growth are true and that they will work in any church that wants to grow. Find new methods to apply these principles and then watch and see what the Lord will do.

GREAT COMMISSION
RESEARCH JOURNAL
2022, Vol. 14(1) 101-104

Book Review

You Found Me

By Rick Richardson
Downers Grove, IL: InterVarsity Press, 2019
279 pages
USD $24.99

Reviewed by: David C. Thiessen. David serves as Executive Pastor at Mountain View Church in Fresno, CA. He is a Doctor of Ministry student in Church Growth at the Talbot School of Theology at Biola University.

You Found Me by Rick Richardson represents a genre of books meant to bring a positive, hopeful message of balance to the wide range of somewhat discouraging monographs regarding the state of the church and of Christianity that are on the market today. Based on extensive research, the author contends that there is good reason to be optimistic regarding the opportunity to reach the unchurched. The hopeful title is followed by a lengthy subtitle that summarizes the contents of the book: "New Research on How Unchurched Nones, Millennials, and Irreligious are Surprisingly Open to Christian Faith." The author's stated goal is to provide "a strong biblical foundation and best practices from congregations that are effectively reaching people and having an impact in their communities" (18).

Richardson is the director of the Billy Graham Center Institute and a professor at Wheaton College. He has extensive experience as a researcher, and this book draws on a number of studies done in partnership with Lifeway Research. Two thousand unchurched people were surveyed to find out their views on American churches and their responsiveness to various forms of Christian outreach. In addition, 3,000 congregations across the country were surveyed to discover their rate of conversion growth. The most effective of these churches, defined as "top-ten-percent churches" (16) were subject to more in-depth research, including interviews of their pastors and formerly unchurched members. Finally, the results of a "small church evangelism" study representing 1,500 churches with under 250 attenders were included in the research findings (16).

You Found Me is divided into three sections. In part one, "Recovering a Missional Imagination", popular myths regarding the current state of the church and the receptivity of unchurched individuals are examined. The four major myths are: 1) America is becoming non- or anti-Christian; 2) Millennials are leaving the church at an alarmingly high rate; 3) the church in America will disappear in a generation; and 4) trust in the church is at an all-time low (34). What the data actually shows is that the overall percentage of self-identified Christians is declining by one percent annually while those specifically self-identifying as evangelicals have added 2.4 million to their ranks since 2007 (41). Among Millennials that leave the church, many still identify as Christian and expect that they will return to the church in future. Approximately one third of those who have left the church identify the issue of "lost trust," but a majority cite other reasons including a change in circumstances and loss of relevance (46).

Having offered some helpful corrections to these prevalent myths, the author then presents positive news that half of the unchurched people surveyed in his research indicated that they would be open to an invitation to attend a church service or church-related activity. Furthermore, fully one third of those who do not currently attend church expect that they will attend church in the future. This increases to fully 40 percent for unchurched Millennials (71). In light of these statistics, the author contends that "the greatest challenge to congregations is not the shifting or secularizing culture but a discouraged, pessimistic, secularizing, or silent church" (85). As churches embrace a new, positive narrative regarding the receptivity of the unreached, they begin to rekindle a missional imagination. To further this change the author proposes the encouragement of "conversion communities." They are defined as churches that are growing by at least five percent per year, have at least ten percent of their attendance made up of people who have committed to Christ in that year, and have outreach and witness integrated into every ministry of the church (109).

In part two of *You Found Me* the first major ingredient for a conversion community, missional leadership, is explained. Missional leaders are identified as those who lead by example, prioritizing the cultivation of friendships with the unchurched and making the most of their unique opportunities as pastors at weddings, funerals and other public and private events (123). They also promote the multiplication of missional leaders by celebrating outreach, telling stories of mission, and keeping their direct disciples accountable for their own missional activities. This section is short, offering only two chapters; but it can be easily supplemented by many other books that focus solely on the development of missional leaders.

In part three the second ingredient of a conversion community -- the missional congregation -- is explored. Almost 100 pages of the book are given to the practical development of such churches with a focus on the importance of service, invitation and hospitality. The good news regarding the receptivity of the unchurched presented in part one is applied to the local church with the goal of creating a culture of invitation. Richardson asserts that, "The key to reaching lost people is through the relational networks they have with people they trust," and he acknowledges the foundational contribution of Donald McGavran, noting that, "Relationship are the bridges of God" (193). Various types of invitations are suggested including invitations to spiritual conversation, worship services, small groups, service opportunities and ultimately, commitment to Christ (204).

The chief strength of this book is its foundation of extensive research. Based on information from some 4,500 churches surveyed for various research projects, it represents an unusually comprehensive survey. The findings are presented in clear graphs and pie charts, the conclusions are persuasive, and the replacement of doomsday myths with cautiously optimistic realism is a much-needed corrective in the evangelical world. It is unfortunate that crisis headlines sell, but facts and truth are the best antidote and this book provides an ample supply.

Perhaps the most striking insight from the data presented is the relative openness of unchurched people to an invitation to attend church or a church-related activity. This good news is paired with the invitational culture that the author observes in the top-ten-percent churches that he interviews. Of the ten most predictive factors for so-called conversion communities the top factor was a culture of invitation and three of the remaining nine factors were related to the practice of extending regular, personal invitations to the unchurched (110). Because the prevalent myths regarding receptivity have suggested that people are no longer open to invitations to church, this counter-narrative has the potential to reinvigorate Christians, enabling them to see their circle of influence as being relatively receptive to Christianity and to the local church.

Another strength of this book is its collection of illustrative stories showing how conversion communities effectively reach out to the unchurched, largely through individual relationships, one-on-one spiritual conversations, and multiple individual invitations. The stories show how simply relational evangelism works in real life, and how a personal invitation offered at the right time in a person's life can lead to miraculous life-change in Christ. Refreshingly, most of the stories conclude with a credible, evangelical conversion story with the gospel of Jesus Christ being clearly explained, understood and received. It is also remarkable to note that in at least three of the outreach stories shared, children were inviting their parents to church!

Finally, the highlighting of building a hospitable culture makes this book a valuable resource. It points out that congregations make a mistake by, "expecting unchurched visitors to feel welcome through the same experience that draws church insiders to their services and ministries" (213). The author points out how churchy language and unexplained biblical references that seem perfectly normal to Christians can appear bewildering to the unchurched. He believes that taking the time to think through all that we do publicly in worship services can go a long way to helping guests feel more welcome at our churches.

One of the problems with Richardson's premise is the qualifying requirements for his conversion communities. While research often requires some arbitrary guidelines, this one seems an extraordinarily high bar to clear, especially his expectation that at least ten percent of the church's attendance be made up of new converts from the prior calendar year. There are very few churches in America that would qualify, especially post-Covid.

There are also are some potential challenges embedded in the culture of the unchurched world and in the local church that may make some of the author's strategies difficult to implement. For example, community engagement is recommended as a key activity for missional congregations but outside of local schools and a very select number of remaining community institutions, the increasing individualism and disconnectedness of our culture may make community engagement difficult. Books like Putman's (2001) *Bowling Alone* have documented this decline and the local church may find itself pushing uphill in an effort to reverse the decline.

A final critique is that, given the apparent declining priority of a culture of corporate prayer in the local church today, the author's discussion of prayer for the lost may reflect this trend more than challenge it. In the one-page discussion of the role of prayer in missional congregations, it appears that prayer is viewed as a tool to increase missional awareness rather than as an actual means of outreach. While it is true that praying for opportunities to engage the unchurched will typically increase our awareness of Spirit-produced opportunities, this should be seen only as a helpful byproduct of prayer rather than its main purpose.

Aside from these mild concerns, *You Found Me* is an excellent contribution to the study of church growth today. This book is an excellent resource for pastors, church staff and church leadership teams. Helpful discussion questions are offered at the end of each chapter and practical application steps make this a resource that local churches can put to use immediately. The author has done a great service to the church, giving fact-based reasons for evangelistic hope and genuine optimism in an increasingly secular culture.

Reference

Putnam, R. (2001). Bowling Alone: The collapse and revival of American Community. New York: Touchtone.

GREAT COMMISSION
RESEARCH JOURNAL
2022, Vol. 14(1) 105-107

Book Review

The Innovation Crisis: Creating Disruptive Influence in the Ministry You Lead

By Ted Esler
Chicago, IL: Moody Publishers, 2021
288 pages
USD $13.59

Reviewed by Joseph W. Handley, Jr. president of Asian Access and catalyst for leader development with the Lausanne Movement.
https://www.asianaccess.org/senior-leaders/bio-joe-handley.

Esler's latest book on innovation in ministry is both timely and challenging for those of us serving in churches and in the missionary field. He gives a clarion call for Christian workers to break out of the current molds and attempt bold new ventures for God's kingdom. As he aptly notes, "I believe we have a crisis of innovation among ministries today... The Christian worldview is waning in Western society. The enormous cultural and religious shifts around us are making decades of ministry irrelevant (258)." This passion for innovation drives Esler to exhort Christian leaders to follow William Carey's example to:

Expect great things from God, [and] attempt great things for God.

The Innovation Crisis does a masterful job of weaving theory with practical, real life modern examples of how innovation can be attempted. Esler integrates solid theoretical principles and illustrates them with stories giving both context and inspiration for better understanding and clear pathways for implementing these innovations within one's own ministry context. He outlines five different avenues for approaching innovation that are quite helpful. Creatively drawing from William Carey, the shoemaker, he calls these five pathways "The Shoemaker Rules."

The first pathway involves "seeing a problem worth solving" (ch. 2). Esler outlines the importance of finding gaps in ministry that we can creatively try to tackle. He identifies the importance of having a mission statement that helps focus an organization or an individual. And, if leaders find that creativity does not emerge naturally, Esler suggests a "blue ocean strategy" to open new vantage points of what may be possible.

The next shoemaker rule is "riding the wave of existing innovation" (ch. 3). In this pathway, collaboration, stacking, platforms, and scale are introduced as viable means for tackling the challenges identified. All of these are proven approaches in business and have value that can be deployed to strengthen a ministry.

Third is a "bias to action"' (ch. 4) where Esler outlines various myths about innovation to try to shake people from the assumption that only certain types of leaders can innovate. He shares practical examples of experimenting with projects and bringing incremental change that many will find helpful. Since few are actually true innovators, as he explains, these experiments and incremental steppingstones provide ample means for those struggling to move forward.

The next pathway, "empathize, then strategize" (ch. 5), provides one of the most useful methodologies that many may be unaware of. Design Thinking is introduced as a vehicle for helping leaders to unleash new solutions and brainstorm valuable perspectives and insights to address challenges. This five-stage process is the one used by renown groups like IDEO and leaders will find that it is well worth investigating in order to bring innovation to their ministries.

Finally, Esler challenges the leader to "think big" (ch. 5) and tackle "wicked problems." These are problems that are so difficult that they may seem impossible to even attempt. By stretching to large-sized challenges, one is forced to think outside of boxes and attempt things, much like William Carey did, that are beyond imagination.

These shoemaker rules are then followed by several chapters that encourage readers to identify targets and step into the role of an innovative leader. Again, several practical examples and creative ventures are shared to help the reluctant take up the challenge. With all of this, the book lives up to its billing, as Carey Nieuwhof ably notes in the foreword: "You'll encounter some super sharp observations, innovative thinking, really tough questions, challenging ideas, and a call to innovate that will hopefully make you (and me) uncomfortable enough to do something risky that might not work."

While I have great appreciation for what *The Innovation Crisis* reveals, I would be remiss not to offer a few critiques or suggestions for further study. Esler does a fantastic job digging into the theories and laying out the groundwork for ministries to look at innovation. Pointing to the likes of Peter Drucker and Everett Rogers as foundational to this genre, as Esler does, is important. However, I was surprised that Drucker's (1985) own book on innovation, *Innovation and Entrepreneurship*, was not mentioned. I also believe the research on *Immunity to Change* (Kegan and Lahey, 2009) could have been explored and would have added significant value to the overall excellent work that Esler conducted. Another concurrent entry in this field well worth reviewing is Doug Paul's *Ready or Not*. It complements Esler's contribution.

Additionally, while the book includes biblical passages at the front of each chapter and a few theological reflections throughout, exploring a more robust theology of creation or innovation could help Christian leaders understand the importance of pursuing innovation. I will conclude by praising Esler for his thoughtful and important insight shared below. This shows his humility and wisdom in making this outstanding contribution for us as ministry leaders:

> A final warning is that, as Christians, we must recognize timeless truth that is not subject to innovation. We are not going to further enhance the gospel with innovation. We are not going to solve the problem of sin through innovation. Managerial practices will not replace biblical models of ministry. It is within the limits and framework of Scripture that we will find human flourishing. Innovation has an application for ministry but it is not the kingdom of God. (38)

With this brilliant caveat, Esler should be commended for providing a rich resource for the Church and Mission worlds, inspiring and challenging us to boldly innovate to honor our Lord's commission and better serve him in that venture.

To further your understanding, you may also enjoy the IQ test Esler provides. He notes that it is unproven as an instrument, but I did find it insightful, and it could be helpful in your journey toward innovation: http://theinnovationcrisis.com/iqtest/

References

Drucker, P. (1985). Innovation and Entrepreneurship. New York: Routledge.

Kegan, R. & Lahey, L. (2009). Immunity to Change. Boston, MA: Harvard Business School.

GREAT COMMISSION
RESEARCH JOURNAL
2022, Vol. 14(1) 109-111

Book Review

Evangelism in a Skeptical World: How to Make the Unbelievable News About Jesus More Believable

By Sam Chan
Grand Rapids, MI: Zondervan, 2018
288 pages
USD $24.99, Hardcover

Reviewed by Cameron D. Armstrong, author of *Listening Between the Lines: Thinking Missiologically about Romanian Culture* (2018). Cameron (PhD, Biola University) serves with the International Mission Board in Bucharest, Romania, where he teaches at the Bucharest Baptist Theological Institute. Cameron's research interests include orality, theological education, and Romania.

The word "evangelism" evokes strong feelings for most. For many Christians, evangelism is frightening and unnatural, even though many believe that it ought to be a defining mark of a true believer. Enter Sam Chan - an Asian Australian evangelist with a Ph.D. from Trinity Evangelical Divinity School. Based on his experiences in personal and large gathering evangelism encounters, Chan's *Evangelism in a Skeptical World* addresses Christians' fears in a highly practical and theologically sound manner.

Chan's book is divided into ten chapters. Beginning with a "theology of evangelism," the chapters survey such topics as evangelism among postmoderns, contextualization, crafting a gospel presentation, delivering evangelistic talks, and apologetics. Throughout the book, Chan reminds us that evangelism cannot be defined by methods, since there are many different evangelistic methods in the Bible. Instead, evangelism is defined by the message of the gospel. Chan therefore explains that evangelism is "our human effort of proclaiming the message of the gospel" and involves trusting God to use our efforts for his purposes (24). One of the pitfalls Christians face in evangelism training, according to Chan, is the effort to discover a one-size-fits-all approach. Chan spends considerable time evaluating previous attempts at such methods, such as the Four Spiritual Laws (popular in the United States) and Two Ways to Live (popular in Australia). While these proved excellent evangelism tools in previous generations, these methods may not resonate with non-believers in the skeptical, postmodern world. In engaging postmoderns, whose plausibility structures are informed more from their community and experiences than cognitive data, better approaches might involve inviting non-believers into your community and sharing stories from your own life and from the Bible. In doing so, Christians will better understand what non-believers are truly longing for (what Chan calls their "existential cry") and then be able to show how life with Jesus Christ best completes their "cultural storyline" (163).

The book possesses myriad strengths, yet I will mention only three. First, Chan balances well his rigorous theology of evangelism with cultural sensitivity. He has clearly thought deeply on both sides to present a work of "critical contextualization" (to use language Chan himself borrows from missiologist Paul Hiebert). Second, readers will find Chan's insertion of "storytelling the gospel" both informative and freeing. Instead of trying to memorize evangelism methods, Chan demonstrates the power of using stories from both the Bible and the Christian's life, especially among skeptics in the postmodern West. Third, readers from North America especially will find Chan's chapters on understanding postmoderns and cultural hermeneutics worthwhile. Not only does Chan elucidate how postmodernism challenges traditional evangelism methods, but he also exposes how a society's "cultural texts" often point to biblical metaphors.

As for weaknesses, I will also mention three. First, Chan does not address the reality that often Christians may not have close non-Christian friends. Instead, Chan merely assumes they do. Chan's strategy of inviting non-believers out for coffee a few times and then over for dinner for deeper conversation is indeed a brilliant idea, yet may be unrealistic if the Christian has no non-believing friends in the first place. Second, while describing the need for evangelism to use both guilt and shame language, Chan asserts that the apostles in the New Testament only used guilt language when speaking with Jews and shame language when engaging the pagan Greeks. Even a cursory reading of the book of Romans will show this not to be the case, underscored by recent works such as Jackson Wu's *Reading Romans with Eastern Eyes*. Third, Chan's emphasis on topical preaching as more relevant in today's world may ruffle more than a few feathers among the evangelical establishment. Even though Chan argues the point thoroughly, such an argument may find few adherents in circles committed to exposition as the homiletic apex.

Yet these are minor weaknesses that do not detract from the book's message. For brevity, cultural understanding, and winsomeness, Chan is to be commended for producing a truly helpful guide. Indeed, I have come across few evangelism resources more practical than *Evangelism in a Skeptical World*. Church leaders in the Global West, including North America, will find encouragement, challenge, and practical tips for equipping Christians to neither fear nor ignore the biblical command to evangelize.

References

Wu, J. (2019). *Reading Romans with Eastern Eyes*. Downers Grove, IL: IVP Academic.

GREAT COMMISSION
RESEARCH JOURNAL
2022, Vol. 14(1) 113-115

Book Review

The Life and Impact of Phil Parshall: Connecting with Muslims

Edited by Kenneth Nehrbass and Mark Williams
Littleton, CO: William Carey Publishing, 2021
108 pages
USD $11.99

Reviewed by J. Stephen Jester. Stephen has a PhD in intercultural studies from the Assemblies of God Theological Seminary and spent over twenty-five years working among Muslims in West Africa. He currently teaches Christian Worldview and Missions courses at Grand Canyon University.

Arriving as a new missionary to West Africa in the early 1990s, I experienced an array of new sights and sounds as a reminder that my new home was completely foreign to my experiences. The first morning in Africa, the "call to prayer" reverberated from the local mosque with an enchanted summons for devotees to attend morning prayer. We were filled with a passion for the place and people; but we had little understanding of Islam, the five pillars, and the impact of the religion to the daily lives of Muslims. It was in this context I first met Phil Parshall. I needed someone to serve as a guide and mentor for this young naïve missionary and I found his wisdom and discernment a beacon that helped me, time and again, to find my way. I was not privileged to meet him in person, but encountered him through the pages of *New Paths in Muslim Evangelism, Bridges to Islam, Beyond the Mosque,* and *The Cross and the Crescent*. I found these works practical and insightful for the challenges faced in my context. I found hope that I too could enter the culture and present the Gospel in contextually appropriate ways that remained faithful to the truth of Scripture.

The Life and Impact of Phil Parshall provides much more insight into Phil

Parshall by those who knew him and were shaped in some way by his experience and scholarship. This short book is a fitting tribute to the man whose life and thought influenced many cross-cultural workers in Islamic contexts. Edited by Kenneth Nehrbass and Mark Williams, the book is divided into seven distinct chapters with unique contributions from those who knew and engaged the ideas proposed by Parshall. Each author engages Parshall's thought, offering his or her own contribution to his ideas.

In chapter one, Gary Corwin provides a fitting review of Parshall's life and legacy with a narrative of his formative years and conversion. Early exposure to world missions developed in him an inner compulsion to perceive culture and people through God's point of view. The Muslim world was calling; and this led him to a significant phase of missionary work in Bangladesh. That context became the catalyst for developing his focus on "contextualization to local and Muslim patterns of life, but with great care not to cross lines into anything that was not biblically permissible" (9). It laid the foundation for *New Paths in Muslim Evangelism* and many of his additional scholarly publications. Corwin's summary of Parshall's legacy highlights his contribution to Muslim contextualization, his scholarly publications and teaching, his willingness to contest an idea with humility while remaining open to all perspectives, and his initiation of "a movement of church mobilization for outreach to Muslims" (13).

Chapter two provides personal reflections from Kevin Higgins, one of those students of Parshall's who never sat under his teachings but was profoundly influenced by him nonetheless. Higgins describes Parshall as an innovator who allowed others to follow in his footsteps and even take his ideas in new directions. He learned from Parshall to cross frontiers in "probing the consequences of contextualizing so-called Christian 'forms'...in order to allow truly biblical 'functions' to flourish in a cross-cultural setting" (18). This happens when one listens well to what Muslims think and feel with a posture of humility toward the other.

Miriam Adeney reminds readers in chapter three that culture still matters. It mattered for Parshall in identifying with Islamic culture. It mattered to the early Church. Her lens for contextualizing within any culture comes straight from the Scriptures to emphasize that Paul and the early faith community wrestled with the same cultural adaptation issues and its consequences. It was important then and even more imperative today. While globalizing influences may alter certain aspects of the worldview and behaviors of a people group, sensitivity to the local culture remains an essential focus of living out the *Missio Dei*. For Parshall, adapting to the local was crucial. "Only one offense should intrude: the true offense of the gospel, the cross that is a scandal and stumbling block to people's pride in every culture. Beyond that, Christian witness should adapt" (40).

In chapter four, Enoch Jinsik Kim uses Parshall's humble contextualization as his approach to Muslim Background Believers (MBB) in urban contexts. The challenge he considers is how they negotiate multiple identities in their social networks and the implications of these to evangelists working with these new converts. He uses sociological theory to consider the roles and positions people hold in their various communities. Negotiating multiple identities in these multiple roles can create identity confusion, leading to what Kim refers to as a "fuzzy zone" where they are working through role ambiguities that do not specifically fit traditional categories of Christian identity. This in turn leads to multiple challenges for those working in these communities. As a way forward, Kim offers some models for discipling MBBs through the journey.

Many barriers confront missionaries in contextualizing the Gospel to Muslims. In Chapter five, Harley Talman builds upon Parshall's "new paths" to reaching Muslims through the lens of a case study in which the author identifies three obstacles: cultural differences, religious identity, and communal decision dynamics. Incarnational witness, an emphasis on the Kingdom of God (as opposed to Christianity as merely a religion), and group consensus were all means of overcoming the identified challenges.

Joseph Williams revisits the debate involving the C1-C6 Spectrum in chapter six as he looks at the concerns of syncretism in each of the C categories. He asks whether these categories are descriptive or prescriptive. At the heart of the issues expressed by Parshall, as well as by Williams and other missiologists, is the opaque distinction between religion, culture, and identity that cannot simply be reduced to a simple definition and categorization. This includes cautions to be considered that would hinder Muslim Background Believers from analyzing and evaluating their faith community under Christ's Lordship.

Finally, John Jay Travis uses his experiences in Southeast Asia to demonstrate that Parshall's emphasis on lifestyle and modelling remains one of the most relevant aspects of engaging with Muslims. Living cross-culturally as authentic incarnational agents necessitates relationship building, hospitality to the other, adapting to the culture in food and dress, and most importantly, walking daily with the Spirit through a robust personal discipleship.

I found this book a delight to read as it gave me additional insights into the ways Parshall has influenced missiology - and specifically, contextualization among Muslims. Each chapter provides more detail and substance on the man, his passion, and his lasting legacy regarding the debate on appropriate contextualization and incarnational mission. I highly recommend this work to students and instructors alike.

GREAT COMMISSION
RESEARCH JOURNAL
2022, Vol. 14(1) 117-118

Book Review

Towards a Pentecostal Theology of Praxis: A Case Study

By John Mark Robeck
New York: Lexington Books/Fortress Academic, 2021
171 pages
USD $74.02

Reviewed by Norlan Josué Hernández. Norlan is a Ph.D. Candidate at Cook School of Intercultural Studies at Biola University. He lives in Los Angeles, California and has Nicaraguan roots.

In a day and age when the concept of decolonization is garnering considerable attention in various disciplines across the academy, John Mark Robeck's book, *Towards a Pentecostal Theology of Praxis: A Case Study*, is a timely addition. Although not explicitly a decolonial effort, it does serve as a resource that highlights the epistemological realities in a Latin American context that shed light on the task of decolonizing theology.

The purpose of the book is, in the words of Robeck himself, an "inquiry related to the development of a formal Pentecostal theology of praxis" (p. 9) through a mixed methods approach that includes qualitative and theoretical components. Regarding the qualitative elements, Robeck investigates "a group of churches that operate in the country of El Salvador, and in conjunction with a faith-based NGO named ENLACE" (10). As for the theoretical aspect, Robeck relies on the frameworks of Liberation Theology and Pentecostal Theology. Through these means, Robeck provides an insightful assessment of the intersection of these two theological camps as experienced in churches actively engaged in social projects. Robeck's work also provides both theoretical and practical observations that are useful in giving direction for a Pentecostal theology of praxis.

The book is structured around six chapters. In the introduction, Robeck lays the foundation for the study, which includes the similarities between Liberation Theology and Pentecostalism, an argument against the notion that Pentecostalism is "so futuristically orientated that they neglect the here and now all together" (7), and a brief description of ENLACE's work.

Chapter one utilizes Gustavo Gutierrez's seminal work, *A Theology of Liberation,* to describe elements that will then be correlated to Pentecostalism. Robeck also highlights various concepts developed by Pentecostal scholars that make the case for the consideration of the similarities between Pentecostalism and Liberation Theology, which set the stage for a Pentecostal theology of praxis.

The Salvadoran Pentecostal context is described in chapter two. This chapter includes a brief historical account of growth of Pentecostalism in El Salvador, an introduction to various important ecclesial leaders and their contributions, and a brief recapitulation of the various denominational movements in the country. Each of these concepts proves to be imperative for understanding the Pentecostal movement in El Salvador today.

Chapter three describes the three churches and their respective pastors that make up the case study. The story depicts the interrelationships between the churches' lived experiences and their engagement with the social context surrounding the churches.

In chapter four, Robeck takes on the task of evaluating the content of sermons and hymns in order to articulate how Pentecostal praxis is communicated within the churches in the case study.

While the author utilizes multiple forms of data (i.e., theoretical and qualitative), the book has two gaps. First, the content does not account for women's roles in church and in social engagement efforts. While it may be true that within the Salvadoran context men are often the ones holding formal leadership positions, women are not completely detached from the work being done within and outside the church. Second, although Robeck provides examples of how experience informs pastors' theology in El Salvador, he does not explicitly explain how this process works. There is an epistemological assumption being made. Hence, an epistemological evaluation of this process might be helpful in providing greater clarity concerning the specific context from which the development of a Pentecostal theology of praxis is taking place.

Nonetheless, Robeck's work is a valuable asset for the body of literature that sheds light on theology and ministry in the context of El Salvador. It is a great resource for organizations that seek to serve communities in El Salvador and neighboring countries. Missionaries may find this book to be an invaluable tool as they work within this context. This book is also a great resource for higher education institutions in that it provides helpful insights that can be used in a variety of courses, such as global Christianity, Latin American Christianity, missions, pastoral ministry, contextualization, and Latin American theology, to name a few.

GREAT COMMISSION
RESEARCH JOURNAL
2022, Vol. 14(1) 119-121

Book Review

When Everything is Mission

By Denny Spitters and Matthew Ellison
Bottomline Media, 2017
146 pages
USD $9.99

Reviewed by Kenneth Nehrbass. Kenneth earned a BA in classical civilization from the University of California, Irvine, an M.Div. from Anderson School of Theology, an MA in education from Biola University, and a Ph.D. in intercultural studies from Biola University. He is an associate professor of global studies for Rawlings School of Divinity at Liberty University.

Spitters and Ellison – both pastors and mission leaders– have written the most comprehensive argument for prioritism to date (other than the New Testament itself). The prioritism-holism issue is an "in house" debate among evangelicals that dates back to the early 19th century. The central question is whether proclamation of the gospel (especially among the unreached) should take priority in the missionary task. Spitters and Ellison argue that not only does cross-cultural proclamation of the gospel take priority, it is the only activity that can truly be called "missions." Yes, missionaries do a lot of things, but the "bullseye," they say, is reaching the unreached.

Some of the recent watering down of the definition of missions has to do with a postmodern distaste for clarifying any terms. Spitters and Ellision critique David Bosch's deconstructionist claim that "missions" is impossible to define because it has gone through major paradigm shifts. Further, they argue that Christopher Wright's well-intentioned project to find a missional hermeneutic ends up conflating "missions" with the missio Dei. What we need, they argue, is clarity.

Getting the definition of missions right is more than semantics. Their thesis is that how the church thinks about missions impacts the way it engages in missions. (Ideas have consequences). There are financial, ethical, and spiritual implications when "missions becomes everything." From a financial standpoint, if missions is "anything the church feels called to do," it will (and does) devote almost all of its budget to local causes. The financial issue becomes an ethical one: The authors give several recent, prominent examples where churches diverted money that was given for the missions fund to pay the utility bills and salaries of the staff. But if missions is everything, what is to keep the church from going down this slippery slope? And from a spiritual standpoint, if anything that a church is passionate about can be called "mission(s)", then the task of reaching the unreached will be the last priority for many congregations, leaving hundreds of millions of people in spiritual darkness.

But will an emphasis on conversion detract from laudable efforts like social action? Not at all. The authors briefly explore Robert Woodberry's landmark work that showed conversionary Christianity has been responsible for much social uplift throughout the world. They also take time to problematize the accusation that missions has ridden on the coattails of colonialism.

The authors define missions as inviting people from all tribes, tongues and nations to worship the Lamb (Rev 7:9). (Note that the connection between missions and worship, influenced by John Piper, is woven throughout the book). With such a narrow classification for the term "missions," Spitters and Ellison subvert the notion that "everyone is a missionary" (they give a number of famous permutations of this meme). Yet they heartily agree that all Christians have a role to play in missions. In fact, this may seem counterintuitive, but their high regard for the special place of missions actually drives their high ecclesiology: The Church is essential to the entire missionary task, from identifying potential missionaries, to training them, to sending them out, to keeping them on the field, and to holding them accountable to their work. Therefore, revering the task of missions does not lead to disparaging other aspects of the church. The authors clearly champion other Christian engagements, such as youth ministry, social action, and Christian radio. They are just fans of clarity: Call youth work "youth work" and call social action "social action." Such precision enables the church to be honest about where its money is going, and what its personnel are up to.

The book works as the main text for an introductory course on missions, because it is more than an apologia for prioritism: It traces the history of the Protestant missions era; it provides a biblical theology of missions; it introduces readers to important missiologists; and it introduces missiological concepts like ethne, unreached people groups, and a conscious, eternal hell for unbelievers. Additionally, because this text brings together a number of voices who have argued for prioritism, it could also be used in higher level missiology courses, where students could critique prioritists' arguments.

If your senior pastor or elders have been lumping the church's various outreach (and in-reach) programs under the moniker of missions, this book could help transform their understanding of the precious term "missions," and may even give them a fresh vision for reaching the unreached.

CALL FOR PAPERS

Knox Fellowship Awards 2022

RESEARCH IN EVANGELISM

Sponsored by the Great Commission Research Network and Knox Fellowship

Purpose:
The Great Commission Research Network and Knox Fellowship are sponsoring the 2022 Call for Papers and awards for Research in Evangelism, with winning and outstanding papers to be considered for publication in the Fall 2022 issue of the *Great Commission Research Journal*. The goal of the competition is to compile and disseminate research that serves to help churches fulfill the Great Commission (Matt. 28:18-20).

Submissions (Due May 15):
Papers should present original research not yet published relevant to the field of evangelism. They should be 3000-7000 words and in APA format. Submissions should be emailed by May 15, 2022, to David Dunaetz, editor of the *Great Commission Research Journal*: ddunaetz@apu.edu

Publication and Awards:
Four $500 awards will be granted to papers in any of the following categories. **Students are especially encouraged to submit papers.**

1) **Theological Research**
   -Focusing on developing a biblical theology of some theme relevant to contemporary evangelism.
2) **Empirical Research**
   -Reporting quantitative research (e.g., hypothesis testing with survey data) or qualitative research (e.g., interviews to answer a research question) on a topic relevant to evangelism.
3) **Case Studies**
   -A description and analysis of evangelism in a specific context (e.g., a local church).

The most valuable contributions will be considered for publication in the Fall 2022 issue of the *Great Commission Research Journal*. If there are a sufficient number of valuable contributions, they may be published in a book.

GREAT COMMISSION RESEARCH NETWORK

(formerly: The American Society for Church Growth)

OFFICERS

President:
Dr. Jay Moon
Professor of Church Planting and Evangelism
Asbury Theological Seminary
Email: jay.moon@asburyseminary.edu

First Vice President:
Dr. Brad Ransom
Chief Training Officer
Director of Church Planting
Free Will Baptist North American Ministries
Email: brad@nafwb.org

Treasurer:
Ben Penfold
Chief Executive Officer
Penfold & Company

GREAT COMMISSION RESEARCH NETWORK

greatcommissionresearch.com

MEMBERSHIP

What is the Great Commission Research Network?

The Great Commission Research Network (GCRN) is a worldwide and professional association of Christian leaders whose ministry activities have been influenced by the basic and key principles of church growth as originally developed by the late Donald McGavran. Founded by renowned missiologists George G. Hunter III and C. Peter Wagner, the GCRN has expanded into an affiliation of church leaders who share research, examine case studies, dialogue with cutting-edge leaders, and network with fellow church professionals who are committed to helping local churches expand the kingdom through disciple-making.

Who Can Join the GCRN?

GCRN membership is open to all who wish a professional affiliation with colleagues in the field. The membership includes theoreticians, such as professors of evangelism and missions, and practitioners, such as pastors, denominational executives, parachurch leaders, church planters, researchers, mission leaders, and consultants. Some members specialize in domestic or mono-cultural church growth, while others are cross-culturally oriented.

Why Join the GCRN?

The GCRN provides a forum for maximum interaction among leaders, ministries, and resources on the cutting edge of Great Commission research. The annual conference of the GCRN (typically held in March each year) offers the opportunity for research updates and information on new resources and developments, as well as fellowship and encouragement from colleagues in the field of church growth. Membership in the GCRN includes a subscription to the *Great Commission Research Journal* and a discount for the annual conference.

How Do I Join the GCRN?
For further information on membership and the annual conference, please visit greatcommissionresearch.com.

Membership Fees

- One-year regular membership (inside or outside USA) - $59
- One-year student/senior adult membership (inside or outside USA) - $39
- Three-year regular membership (inside or outside USA) - $177
- Three-year senior membership (inside or outside USA) - $117
- Membership includes a subscription to the *Great Commission Research Journal* which is in the process of transitioning to an electronic format.

GREAT COMMISSION RESEARCH NETWORK AWARDS

Donald A. McGavran Award for Outstanding Leadership in Great Commission Research

Normally once each year, the GCRN gives this award to an individual for exemplary scholarship, intellect, and leadership in the research and dissemination of the principles of effective disciple-making as described by Donald A. McGavran. The award recipients to date:

Win Arn	1989	Rick Warren	2004
C. Peter Wagner	1990	Charles Arn	2005
Carl F. George	1991	John Vaughan	2006
Wilbert S. McKinley	1992	Waldo Werning	2006
Robert Logan	1993	Bob Whitesel	2007
Bill Sullivan	1994	Bill Easum	2009
Elmer Towns	1994	Thom S. Rainer	2010
Flavil R. Yeakley Jr.	1995	Ed Stetzer	2012
George G. Hunter III	1996	Nelson Searcy	2013
Eddie Gibbs	1997	J. D. Payne	2014
Gary L. McIntosh	1998	Alan McMahan	2015
Kent R. Hunter	1999	Steve Wilkes	2016
R. Daniel Reeves	2000	Art McPhee	2016
Ray Ellis	2002	Mike Morris	2017
John Ellas	2003	Bill Day	2019

Win Arn Lifetime Achievement Award in Great Commission Research

This award is given to a person who has excelled in the field of American church growth over a long period of time. The award recipients to date:

Eddie Gibbs	2011	Gary McIntosh	2015
Elmer Towns	2012	Kent R. Hunter	2017
George G. Hunter III	2013	Carl George	2019
John Vaughan	2014		

American Society for Church Growth/GCRN Past Presidents

C. Peter Wagner	1986	Ray W. Ellis	1999-00
George G. Hunter III	1987	Charles Van Engen	2001-02
Kent R. Hunter	1988	Charles Arn	2003-04
Elmer Towns	1989	Alan McMahan	2005-06
Eddie Gibbs	1990	Eric Baumgartner	2007-08
Bill Sullivan	1991	Bob Whitesel	2009-12
Carl F. George	1992	Steve Wilkes	2013-14
Flavil Yeakley Jr.	1993	Mike Morris	2015-16
John Vaughan	1994	James Cho	2017-18
Gary L. McIntosh	1995-96	Gordon Penfold	2019-20
R. Daniel Reeves	1997-98		

GREAT COMMISSION RESEARCH NETWORK
SUBMISSIONS

The *Great Commission Research Journal* publishes both peer-reviewed articles reporting original research and reviews of recent books relevant to evangelism and disciple making.

The scope of the journal includes research focusing on evangelism, church planting, church growth, spiritual formation, church renewal, worship, or missions. Articles come from both members and non-members of the Great Commission Research Network and are generally unsolicited submissions, which are welcomed and will be considered for peer-review. There is no charge for submission or publication.

ARTICLES

All submissions should be emailed to the editor, David R. Dunaetz at ddunaetz@apu.edu.

Peer Review Process

Only the highest quality submissions presenting original research within the scope of the journal will be chosen for publication. To ensure this, all articles will go through a peer review process. Articles deemed by the editor to have potential for publication will be sent to reviewers (members of the editorial board or other reviewers with the needed expertise) for their recommendation. Upon receiving the reviewers' recommendations, the author will be notified that the submission was either rejected, that the submission has potential but needs to be significantly revised and resubmitted, that the submission is conditionally accepted if the noted issues are addressed, or that the submission is accepted unconditionally.

Format

Papers should be APA formatted according to the 7th edition of the Publication Manual of the American Psychological Association. Submissions should include a cover page, be double-spaced in Times New Roman, and be between 3,000 and 7,000 words (approximately 10-22 pages) in .docx format. Contact the editor for exceptions to this word count.

In-text references should be in the form (Smith, 2020) or (Smith, 2020, p.100). At the end of the article should be a References section. No footnotes should be used. Minimize the use of endnotes. If endnotes are necessary, more than two or three are strongly discouraged; rather than using Microsoft Word's endnote tool, place them manually before the References section.

Include an abstract of approximately 100-150 words at the beginning of your text.

After the References section, include a short biography (approximately 30 words) for each author.

BOOK REVIEWS

The purpose of our book reviews is to direct the reader to books that contribute to the broader disciple making endeavors of the church. The review (500-2000 words) is to help potential readers understand how the book will contribute to their ministry, especially those in North America or which have a large cross-cultural base. The review should consist of a summary of the contents, an evaluation of the book, and a description of how the book is applicable to practitioners.

Before submitting a book review, please contact the book review editor Ken Nehrbass (krnehrbass@liberty.edu) to either propose a book to be reviewed or to ask if there is a book that needs to be reviewed.

COPYRIGHT

CONTACT INFORMATION

To submit an article or for general questions, contact:
Dr. David Dunaetz, ddunaetz@apu.edu

For questions about book reviews, contact:
Ken Nehrbass, krnehrbass@liberty.edu

Made in the USA
Middletown, DE
11 March 2022

62465007R00073